FROM
SEA
TO
SEA

FROM SEA TO SEA

THE GROWTH
OF THE
UNITED STATES

HAROLD FABER

CHARLES SCRIBNER'S SONS
NEW YORK
Maxwell Macmillan Canada • Toronto
Maxwell Macmillan International
New York • Oxford • Singapore • Sydney

Charles Scribner's Sons Books for Young Readers
Macmillan Publishing Company
866 Third Avenue, New York, NY 10022

Maxwell Macmillan Canada, Inc.
1200 Eglinton Avenue East, Suite 200
Don Mills, Ontario M3C 3N1

Macmillan Publishing Company is part of the
Maxwell Communication Group of Companies.
Second edition
First edition published by Farrar, Straus & Giroux, Inc.
Printed in the United States of America

Library of Congress Cataloging-in-Publication Data
Faber, Harold.
From sea to sea : the growth of the United States / Harold Faber.
—2nd ed.   p.   cm.
Includes bibliographical references (p.   ) and index.
Summary: An account of the territorial growth of the United States from the
Treaty of 1783 to the acquisition of Hawaii in 1959.
ISBN 0-684-19442-2
1. United States—Territorial expansion—Juvenile literature.
2. United States—Territories and possessions—Juvenile literature.
[1. United States—Territorial expansion.]   I. Title.
E179.5.F3   1992   973—dc20   91-43728

For Alice and Margie

Contents

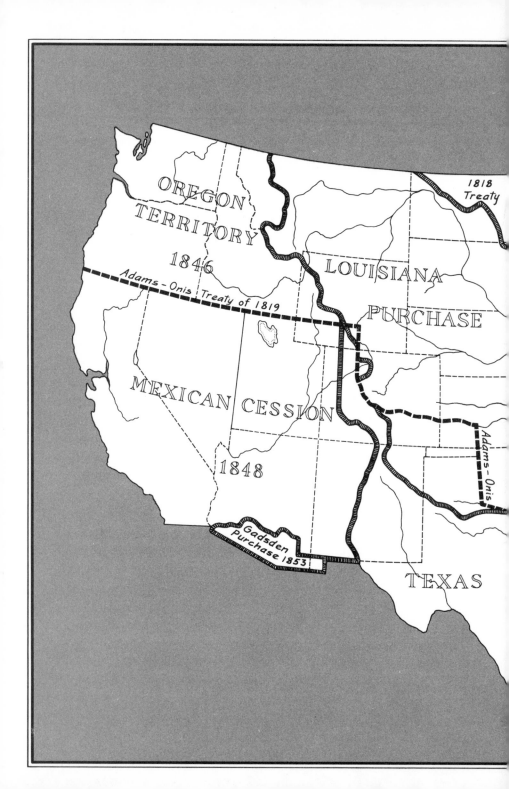

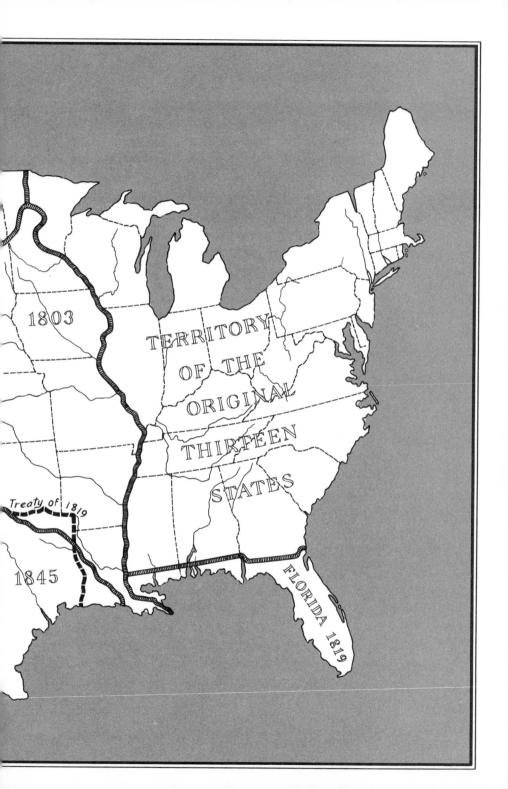

1803

TERRITORY

OF THE

ORIGINAL

THIRTEEN

STATES

Treaty of 1819

1845

FLORIDA 1819

1

The New Nation

ON THE MORNING OF AUGUST 12 in the year 1782 two trou-
bled Americans climbed into a carriage in the Paris suburb
of Passy and set off to visit the court of Louis XVI, king of
France, America's staunch ally in the Revolutionary War. Victory and independence for the thirteen American states were
in sight, and yet here they were, charged with negotiating a
peace treaty with their enemy, England—but actually fighting
a war of words with their friend, France.

One of the men was the distinguished American Benjamin
Franklin, printer, scientist, philosopher, and diplomat, now
seventy-six and ailing, his hair thin and white. Carrying a
crab-apple walking stick, he limped a little, from his recent
attack of the gout. His companion was John Jay, only half his
age, tall, slender, vigorous at thirty-seven, a man of imposing
background. He had been chief justice of New York and a
president of the Continental Congress before being sent
abroad as a diplomat.

For four months now, Franklin had been meeting informally
with various English representatives in the tedious business

of preparing to negotiate the peace. It had been clear since the previous October, when Lord Cornwallis had surrendered his English army to General George Washington at Yorktown, that the American states had won their independence on the battlefield; now it was up to diplomacy to guarantee that freedom in writing.

"Render yourself here as soon as possible," Franklin had written to Jay in Madrid, where for two years he had been trying without success to obtain Spanish loans and Spanish recognition of American independence. So Jay had joined Franklin in Paris in June. The two peace negotiators then began meeting with envoys of England, and almost as often with diplomats from France and Spain, all without much progress.

The two Americans entered the magnificent palace of the French king and were escorted through a labyrinth of ornate corridors to the office of the French foreign minister, Charles Gravier, count de Vergennes, an old friend of Franklin's. There were two problems to be discussed: the text of the English envoy's commission to deal with the Americans and the boundaries of the new nation.

The English agent in Paris charged with negotiating the peace treaty was Richard Oswald, a retired Scottish merchant, a man friendly to Americans and their cause. Just a week earlier, his commission had arrived from London. Clearly the British cabinet had deliberately chosen not to mention the words *United States.* His instructions authorized Oswald to deal with "any commission or commissioners named or to be named by the said colonies or plantations."

Why worry about technicalities? Vergennes asked. As long as independence was made an article of the final treaty of peace, the phraseology was not important. Once Monsieur Oswald received the two men's commissions as plenipotentiaries of the United States, he would in effect have recognized the United States. Thus reasoned the French minister.

Franklin agreed, but the formula did not satisfy Jay.

Vergennes thought the argument was not too important. Had not the American Congress instructed the American negotiators to be governed by the advice and the opinions of their ally, France?

The conference then turned to the boundary question, the line between the United States and the Spanish possessions in North America. At that time, the thirteen states extended from Massachusetts (including what is now the state of Maine) in the north to Georgia in the south. Their eastern boundary was the Atlantic Ocean; the western boundary was not clearly defined. Some of the states claimed lands as far west as the Mississippi River, conflicting with British and Spanish claims, and sometimes with other states.

Here at Versailles the Americans were discussing the boundary question with the French, who no longer had any territorial base in North America. However, Spain, which was not allied with the United States in her war with England, was an ally of France against England. Vergennes was sitting in his own office mediating, in effect, a dispute between his two allies, Spain and the United States. On the basis of his two years in Spain, Jay had defined the issue. The Spanish, he said, desired "to coop us up within the Allegheny Mountains."

Just recently, Jay had conferred with the Spanish minister to France.

"What does the United States expect?" he was asked.

Jay pointed to a map on the table and drew his finger down the Mississippi River.

A few days later he received a map from the Spanish diplomat. The proposed Spanish boundary was marked in red.

It extended from Georgia to the Great Lakes, about five hundred miles east of the Mississippi River.

Jay's response had been immediate, direct, and short: "No." Then the Spanish minister appealed to the French for help.

And so in the office of the French foreign minister, Jay and Franklin expounded the American view to Vergennes and his English-speaking assistant, Gerard de Rayneval. To his subordinates Vergennes had made no secret of his belief that the Americans were asking too much. The French, committed to American independence, had no commitments about the boundaries of the United States. On the contrary, it was part of their foreign policy to confine the new nation within severe limits; it was also part of their policy to help Spain, their other ally, to gain its objectives.

None of this was said outright at the conference, of course, but Rayneval, reflecting Vergennes's position, said the Americans claimed more than they had a right to.

The two Americans left Versailles more dispirited than when they had come.

As their carriage brought them back to Passy, it was clear to Jay that a turning point in American-French relations had been reached. The Americans and the French agreed on American independence, but that was all. For the Americans, their war against the British had been a war for independence and liberty; for the French, the war had been merely another in a long series of imperial rivalries. France had her own interests, some of which the fledgling nation had no part in, such as gaining Gibraltar for Spain; and some of which directly conflicted with the new country, such as fishing rights off Newfoundland.

"There are many reasons that induce me to think that France does not in fact wish to see us treated as independent by other nations until after a peace, lest we should become less manageable in proportion as our dependence on her shall diminish," Jay had written some days earlier to a friend in Philadelphia.

Sitting now in Passy with Franklin, before a fire kindled to warm that gentleman's old bones, Jay once more denounced Vergennes and the French. Why did Vergennes want to hold off recognition of our independence? he asked. And he answered his own question: It was to avoid antagonizing Spain. The key to Spanish intransigence was Gibraltar; they did not want the war to end until they regained it.

"It is true that we owe Spain nothing," Franklin conceded.

France wanted America to remain under her control, Jay went on, until not only their and our objects were attained, but also until Spain should be gratified in her demand to exclude everybody from the Gulf of Mexico and the Mississippi.

Franklin reminded Jay of the instructions they had received from the Continental Congress. The instructions were to govern themselves by the advice and opinion of the king of France and to undertake nothing without the knowledge and consent of the French court.

"Have we any reason to doubt the good faith of the French king?" Franklin asked, and then put a key question to Jay: "Would you deliberately break the instructions of Congress?"

"Unless we violate these instructions, the dignity of Congress will be in the dust," Jay replied without hesitation.

Franklin persisted. "Then you are prepared to break our instructions?"

"If those instructions conflict with the honor and dignity of America, I would break them"—Jay stood up in front of the fireplace and threw his long clay pipe onto the stone hearth— "like this!"

As the pipe shattered, an eventful six weeks that determined the course of American independence and the growth of the United States began.

For the British, too, this was a time for decision. They had faced the reality of American independence for almost a year now but had not yet overcome their reluctance to admit it. In November 1781, when Lord North, then prime minister, learned of Cornwallis's defeat, he said, "O God, it is all over." But King George III was not prepared to recognize the end. In February 1782 a resolution was introduced in the House of Commons to end the war, but it failed by one vote. Five days later, another resolution authorizing the king to make peace passed by nineteen votes.

Then began a complicated political minuet in which the issue of American independence was only one of many factors. The king disliked Lord Rockingham, the new prime minister, and hated Charles James Fox, the foreign minister, both of whom favored independence for the colonies. The king turned instead to the earl of Shelburne, the secretary of state for home, colonial, and Irish affairs. Shelburne, the king hoped, would somehow convince the Americans to listen to terms short of complete independence.

Shelburne's agent, in turn, was Oswald, who wrote: "I always supposed we must satisfy the Americans in such manner as to have a chance to soothe them into neutrality." Oswald first met with Franklin on April 12, 1782, but they really did not get down to particulars until July, after Shelburne became prime minister, in full charge of the negotiations.

On July 10, in a conversation with Oswald, Franklin listed four "necessary" points for peace:

1. Full and immediate independence and the complete withdrawal of British forces

2. Settlement of boundaries

3. Confinement of Canada to where it had been before the Quebec Act of 1774 (in which the southern boundary of Quebec was extended to the Ohio River)

4. Freedom for Americans to continue fishing on the Newfoundland banks

He also listed some "advisable" points: reparation to Americans for damage done by the British; acknowledgment by Parliament of its error in distressing the colonies so much; agreement by each country to give equal privileges to ships and trading of the other; and, lastly, the cession to the United States of the whole of Canada.

While these diplomatic conversations proceeded at a snail's pace during the cold, rainy summer of 1782, other forces were at work, too. Spies, counterspies, agents, and double agents flitted in and out of Paris. At one point the British had three separate negotiators in Paris, each working against the others. There was a spy in the American headquarters, relaying all its confidential information to the British. The French had agents everywhere, and so did the Spanish. For the stakes were high.

Three great imperial powers—a fading Spain, a powerful France, and a Britain torn by internal political dissension— vied with each other and the emerging new Americans for possession of the heartland of North America. No one paid much attention to the rights of a fifth party—the original inhabitants of the land, the American Indians.

In early September some of the complicated machinations of the various imperial powers became known to Jay. First he learned that Rayneval, the chief assistant to the French foreign minister, had left on a secret trip to London. This mission could only mean that France was trying to make a private

agreement with England. Then British agents in Paris carefully brought to Jay's attention a secret letter from a French diplomat in the United States to Vergennes denouncing Americans
for insisting on fishing rights off Newfoundland. And all the
while the French and Spanish ministers continued their pressure on him to give up territory east of the Mississippi.

Jay reacted vigorously. He broke off talks with the Spanish.
More important, now alert to the danger to the United States
if France and England were to reach an agreement without
the Americans, he dispatched an emissary of his own to see
Lord Shelburne. Without consulting his fellow commissioner,
Franklin, Jay advised his emissary to tell Shelburne the following: that England could not count on France to act as a
moderating influence because America "would never treat on
any but an equal footing"; that without an unconditional acknowledgment of independence, peace could not be reason-
ably expected; that it would be impolitic to contest American
claims to the western boundary on the Mississippi; and that
America could not make peace if England denied American
rights to the fisheries off Newfoundland.

At the same time Jay pursued his conversations with
Oswald. A short time before, he had devised a formula to get
around the difficulties of Oswald's commission. He would
accept a preamble to the peace treaty that would describe the
Americans as agents of "the thirteen United States of
America." Oswald agreed.

These two developments—the breaking of the deadlock
over the wording of Oswald's commission and the vigor of
Jay's reaction to the undercover maneuvers—gave urgency to
the mission to London. Jay's agent, Benjamin Vaughan, an
Englishman completely friendly to the Americans, left for
London on September 11 and confronted Shelburne with a

major problem: Would he continue to play politics or would he meet the Americans halfway and conclude the peace?

The British cabinet met and voted to change Oswald's commission as follows: "to treat, consult, and conclude with any commissioner or person vested with equal power by and on the part of the Thirteen United States of America." On September 27 Oswald's commission arrived in Paris and the serious business of negotiating the peace at last got under way.

Just as Franklin had written to Jay months before, Jay now wrote to summon John Adams, the third of the four peace commissioners, who was at the time in Holland. (A fourth, Henry Laurens of South Carolina, had been captured at sea some years before by the British and had been jailed in the Tower of London.) Adams wrote back that he would come as soon as his health permitted. With Franklin ailing, this left only one American negotiator, Jay. On the British side, it was still Oswald, friendly to both Jay and Franklin and personally convinced of the importance of peace for the future of both nations.

The principles of the peace were concluded with astonishing rapidity. Oswald and Jay quickly agreed on the four "necessary" articles outlined by Franklin on July 10. Within a week, working day and night, Jay drafted a provisional peace treaty, which was acceptable to Oswald. It acknowledged American independence, called for the evacuation of British troops and the liberation of prisoners, protected the rights of Americans to fish on the Newfoundland banks, and set the boundaries of the United States as follows:

> East: the St. John River from the Bay of Fundy to Nova Scotia, with the exact line to be determined later; and also the Atlantic Ocean
>
> North: the St. Lawrence River and the forty-fifth degree of north latitude

West: the Mississippi River
South: the thirty-first degree of north latitude (the boundary
of Spanish Florida)

The negotiators were satisfied, but Shelburne was shocked.
The British cabinet directed Oswald to get a better boundary
with Nova Scotia; to reassert British claims to the old
Northwest (the territory above the Ohio River); to recede
from this only if just provisions were made for the Tory
refugees (the British called them Loyalists); to deny rights to
drying fish on Newfoundland; and to call on Americans to
discharge their prewar debts. For the British, the major
unsatisfactory issues were the Loyalists, the debts, and the
fisheries; the boundaries were merely bargaining points. The
British sent another envoy, Henry Strachey, to Paris, to back
up Oswald.

The American negotiating team grew, too. On October 26
John Adams finally arrived in Paris and immediately indicated
his support of Jay's strong stand. At Passy, Franklin, who until
the last maintained that it would be wise to lean on the French
as their instructions prescribed, listened as Adams endorsed
Jay's position of telling the French nothing. In a letter home,
Adams explained his stand: "America has long enough been
involved in the wars of Europe. She has been a football between contending nations from the beginning, and it is easy
to foresee that France and England both will endeavor to
involve us in their future wars."

Finally, Franklin said: "I will go with you and proceed in
the conferences without communicating anything to this
[French] court, and the rather, because they communicate
nothing to us."

The talks actually got under way on October 30 and continued day and night—all, as Adams recalled later, in good

humor. But Adams again stiffened the American attitude. "It is now apparent, at least to Mr. Jay and myself," Adams wrote, "that in order to obtain the western lands, the navigation of the Mississippi and the fisheries, or any of them, we must act with firmness and independence, as well as with prudence and delicacy. With this, there is little doubt that we may obtain them all."

While Oswald sat back, Strachey took over the British side of the negotiations and won a few concessions, too. Adams, for example, persuaded the Americans to accept a proposal whereby Congress would recommend that the states open courts for the recovery of British debts.

On the table before them was a copy of the Map of the British and French Dominions in North America, drawn by Dr. John Mitchell in 1755. "We had before us, through the whole negotiations, a variety of maps; but it was the Mitchell's map upon which was marked out the whole boundary line of the United States," Adams said later. Even though there were many errors in the map, it was the best available at the time. Mitchell's map was the basis for many of the decisions reached in Paris, and it was, therefore, one of the most important maps in American history.

Strachey once more proposed that the western boundary be a line well east of the Mississippi. But the Americans stood firm. "If that line is insisted upon, it is needless to talk of peace," Jay said tartly. "We will never yield on that point."

The boundary dispute, after all, ended rather quickly. Strachey dropped his proposal for a western boundary east of the Mississippi. The Americans in turn offered an alternative to the forty-fifth parallel as the northern boundary: a line through the St. Lawrence and the Great Lakes, an offer that the British accepted as much more favorable for them. There was no dispute about the thirty-first parallel as the southern boundary. But there was an argument about the northeastern border.

British troops still occupied the northern part of Maine (and still held New York, Charleston, and Savannah), but the Americans wanted the northeastern border to run clear up to the St. John River. It did not take much to get them to agree to a more southerly line, the St. Croix River. The British agreed to recognize American fishing rights in Newfoundland, but the Americans refused to budge on the Loyalist issue.

After returning to London for more instructions, Strachey began the last round of talks on November 25, and for three days the arguments were spirited. The British finally yielded on the Loyalist (Tory) issue, and the Americans agreed to refer debt payments to the various states (a face-saving device, since both sides knew nothing would come of it). The fisheries question was settled when both sides agreed on the "liberty" of Americans to fish off Newfoundland (the earlier version of the treaty specified the "right" of Americans).

November 29, 1782, was the key date. On that day Henry Laurens, the fourth American commissioner, finally made his appearance in Paris. (He had been released as a prisoner of war by the British to signal their desire to reach an agreement on the peace treaty.) The British negotiators, faced with accepting the treaty or referring it back to London and thus enduring perhaps months more of haggling, decided to accept it.

The following day, November 30, was set for the signing. The site was Oswald's quarters, the Grand Hotel Moscovite on the rue des Petits Augustins. The two parties compared the documents they had agreed on; they corrected a few minor errors and then sat down at the table to sign. First was Oswald on behalf of the king of England. Then came the Americans in alphabetical order: John Adams, Benjamin Franklin, John Jay, and Henry Laurens.

It was done. The preliminary peace treaty was signed. The war was over. The American colonies had won their independence and had set the geographical bounds of their new nation. But there were still some technicalities in the way of the final peace. The French had to be informed and the British had to ratify the pact.

It fell to Franklin, who understood the French best of all, to convey the information to Vergennes. The French foreign minister was astonished. "The English buy peace rather than make it. Their concessions exceed all that I could have thought possible," he said.

"I am at a loss, sir, to explain your conduct and that of your colleagues on this occasion," Vergennes wrote to Franklin later. "You have concluded your preliminary articles without any communication between us, although the instructions from Congress prescribe that nothing shall be done without the participation of the king."

It was exactly true. The Americans had deliberately concluded the peace treaty without the French, fearing that the French might act contrary to American interests. Without yielding, Franklin once more soothed the French.

"Nothing has been agreed to in the preliminaries contrary to the interests of France," he wrote to Vergennes, "and no peace is to take place between us and England till you have concluded yours. Your observation is, however, apparently just, that in not consulting you before they were signed, we have been guilty of neglecting a point of *bienséance*. But as this was not from want of respect to the king, whom we all love and honor, we hope it will be excused, and that the great work, which has hitherto been so happily conducted, is so

Benjamin West's portrait commemorating the signing of the Treaty of Paris in 1783. (*Left to right*) John Jay, John Adams, Benjamin Franklin, Henry Laurens, and Franklin's grandson, who was secretary to the American commission. The British negotiators refused to pose, so West never finished the portrait. *Courtesy, Winterthur Museum.*

nearly brought to perfection, and is so glorious to his reign, will not be ruined by a single indiscretion of ours."

The French anger, which was more apparent than real, was nothing compared with the turmoil in England. Face to face with the formal loss of the American colonies, the English, from the king on down, hesitated, struggled, and debated before recognizing the facts.

On December 5, 1782, King George III drove to the House of Lords to open a new session of Parliament. Seated on the chair of state, the king read from a scroll, saying that he had tried to reconcile the colonies. He continued, "Finding it indispensable to the attainment of this object, I did not hesitate to go the full length of the powers vested in me and offer to declare them"—and here he paused, obviously embarrassed and distressed—"and offer to declare them free and independent states."

The opposition to the treaty was strong in Parliament, so strong that Shelburne delayed presenting the terms for almost two months. Finally, on February 22, 1783, the House of Commons considered the treaty—and rejected it by a vote of 270 to 190. Shelburne resigned, and Fox became the leader of the British cabinet. In Oswald's place as chief negotiator he appointed David Hartley, one of his own supporters and one of Benjamin Franklin's wide circle of friends.

In Paris, Hartley negotiated with the weary Americans once more. April, May, June, July, August—the talks went on, but no serious changes were made. Finally, on September 3, once again the two negotiating teams sat down, at the Hotel York in the Latin Quarter of Paris, and this time they signed the final treaty of peace. On the same afternoon the British signed treaties with Spain and France. The war really was over.

"We are now friends with England and all mankind," Franklin said. "May we never see another war. For in my opinion, there never was a good war or a bad peace."

The United States was recognized as a free and independent nation. Its boundaries were:

North: the highlands between Maine and Canada, the head of the Connecticut River, the forty-fifth degree of north latitude, the St. Lawrence River, the middle of the Great Lakes, and the river that connects Lake Superior with Lake of the Woods

West: the middle of the Mississippi River

South: the thirty-first degree of north latitude, the middle of the Apalachicola River, the Flint River, and the middle of St. Mary's River

East: the Atlantic Ocean and the middle of the St. Croix River (in Maine)

Every one of these boundary lines, so carefully debated before the peace treaty was signed and so painstakingly drawn on the best maps of the period, raised problems between the two nations almost immediately.

2

The Critical Period

THE KEY TO THE POSTWAR PROBLEMS of the new United States was furs. The skin of the beaver (and to a lesser extent, the muskrat, the raccoon, and the fox) was in great demand in Europe. The fur trade was the biggest industry in North America in the years after the American Revolution. Pelts came into Montreal from the Ohio River, from Hudson's Bay, from as far west as the Rocky Mountains. Indians trapped the fur-bearing animals and sold them to tough, hard-living white men, mostly French, who traveled by canoe into Indian territory.

It was not an easy business, buying furs from the Indians. They wanted iron and hardware, cloth and blankets, guns and powder, beads and trinkets, spices and rum. These goods came into Montreal from Europe and were then jammed into packs weighing about ninety pounds each, so that two packs could be carried on a man's back when necessary.

The packs were transported in large canoes, copied from Indian models, about thirty-five feet long and six feet wide. Each canoe could carry fourteen men and about four tons in cargo. The frame was made of one of the strongest and lightest woods of the northern forests, white cedar. Strips of birchbark, perhaps a quarter of an inch thick, were pressed against the cedar frame and sewn together with a cord made of the roots of juniper or red cedar. The seams were made watertight with pine gum and had to be done over again every day.

There were two routes to the fur country from Montreal. One was up the St. Lawrence River to the Great Lakes and then south to the Ohio River or west to the Rockies. The other, more northerly route, was up the Ottawa River to Lake Huron and then on to Lake Superior. The tiny settlement of Grand Portage on the western shores of Lake Superior was the key transshipment point.

There the hardy French canoemen, called voyageurs, unloaded their trading goods and loaded bales of furs, as many as fifteen hundred skins, for the return trip to Montreal. Then the "winter men" loaded their smaller canoes and paddled upstream to Lake of the Woods and farther north to spend the winter among the Indians and trap more beaver. There were as many as ninety portages between Lake of the Woods and Montreal, at places where the canoes could not navigate the wild rivers. At each portage, a man would take one or two packs of trading goods on his back and tramp or trot to the next water route, stopping to rest every three-quarters of a mile. The canoe would also have to be carried by the men.

The object of all this effort was the amphibious beaver, an animal that made its home in intricate wooden dams built across streams. A full-grown beaver was about forty inches long, covered with thick brown or black fur. Its liver and tail were considered good eating by the Indians and the trappers, but its lush fur was the object of the trade. The winter prime fur, grown by the animal as protection from the cold of the winter months from November to April, was most suitable for the felting process (whereby the fur fibers were pressed and hardened into shape) used in making hats. These tall beaver hats were the mark of fashionable gentlemen all over Europe in the eighteenth and early nineteenth centuries. Fashion led to trade, trade led to exploration, exploration led to conflict and war.

The working men of the fur trade were the Indians and the French. The management was English, at this period the Hudson's Bay Company. Part of the area being tapped was American—the Ohio Valley, the northwest corner of the United States then. The region comprised what is now Wisconsin, Michigan, Illinois, Indiana, Ohio, western Pennsylvania, and western New York. It was the homeland of various Indian tribes (the Delaware, the Shawnee, the Miami, the Wyandot, the Kickapoo, the Potawatomi, and others), which regarded the white men as intruders and fought to keep them out. The only whites who dared enter these lands were fur traders, a few scattered farmers, and soldiers.

The rich Ohio Valley had been the scene of bitter rivalry among the French, the Indians, the British, and the colonists for many years. It was here that General Edward Braddock, accompanied by young George Washington, had been disastrously defeated in 1755. Here were fought some of the bloody battles of the French and Indian War, the war from which Britain emerged as master of the North American continent. In 1768 the British met at Fort Stanwix (now Rome, New York) with the Iroquois Indians, who ceded some of their lands in western New York and Pennsylvania for settlement. In 1774 the British passed the Quebec Act, making the entire Ohio Valley part of Canada. In the Revolutionary War, the British and their Indian allies fought and sometimes massacred scattered settlers in the area.

The British built seven forts there—at Dutchman's Point

and Point-au-Fer, at the northern outlet of Lake Champlain; at Oswegatchie, Oswego, and Niagara, controlling the St. Lawrence River and Lake Ontario; at Detroit, covering Lakes Erie and Huron; and at Mackinac, controlling the entrance to three of the Great Lakes: Huron, Michigan, and Superior. These and one more fort, Fort Erie in Canada, helped protect Canada during the Revolutionary War and served as bases for British attacks on the rebellious colonists.

In the peace treaty that ended the Revolutionary War, the British conceded the entire Ohio Valley to the United States and agreed to evacuate their forts there with "all convenient speed." After the treaty went into effect, however, the British refused to give up the forts and withdraw the redcoats. They claimed, with good reason, that the new United States was not living up to its treaty obligations either. Several of the states were not taking steps to pay monetary debts to the British as guaranteed by the treaty. In addition, returning Loyalists were treated harshly in many of the states. There was an added complication in that the British had yielded to the Americans title to the land of their allies, the Indians, without consulting them, an action that the Indians considered treachery. But the main reason for holding on to the forts was the fur trade.

The problem faced by the British was economic—how to retain the profits of the fur trade. They hoped to do so by creating a buffer Indian state in the Ohio Valley between Canada and the United States and thus continue to do business as usual with the Indians—despite their treaty obligations. The problem faced by the United States was elemental— survival. Could the new nation maintain its independence and the integrity of its borders?

The challenges were ominous. There was no effective national government; the thirteen states were jealous of one another and afraid of a strong central government; the country was ringed by enemies: England to the north and Spain to the south and west. Moreover, within its borders, hostile Indians were on the warpath to protect their lands.

The focus of these conflicts was the Ohio Valley. Since the first colonial grants were made in the seventeenth century, these lands had been claimed by Massachusetts, Virginia, Connecticut, and New York. In 1784–1786, at the insistence of Maryland as the price for adopting the Articles of Confederation of 1781, title to the land was yielded to the federal government.

Two years before the Constitution was adopted, the United States put into effect a far-reaching plan for government there: the Northwest Ordinance of 1787. This provided for the creation of five states when the population of each designated region reached sixty thousand; it barred slavery; and it established a public school system. But settling the rich agricultural region was not simple. Though thirty thousand emigrants a year crossed the Alleghenies, only a handful came into Ohio, mostly at Marietta and Cincinnati, because of the war with the Indians, who were aided by the British.

In 1791 the American general Arthur St. Clair, governor of the Northwest Territory, led two thousand troops, mostly untrained militia, to the Wabash River—and suffered a humiliating defeat near what is now Fort Wayne, Indiana. Little Turtle, chief of the Miami tribe, dispersed the Americans, killing six hundred of them. Facing this disaster and the prospect of more of the same, the new American government, under President Washington, named General (Mad) Anthony Wayne to command in the region.

The British were convinced that the new United States

would not survive this period of ferment. They could see movements to separatism in Vermont (which became the fourteenth state in 1791) and in Kentucky (which became the fifteenth state in 1792). In western Massachusetts, poor farmers had taken up arms in 1786 to prevent courts from foreclosing mortgages (Shays's Rebellion), and four thousand armed troops had been needed to put down the rebellion.

In 1793 another European war broke out. This time, revolutionary France declared war on England, a war that was to last for more than twenty years on and off and profoundly influence the course of American history. The United States was tied to France by a treaty of amity signed in 1778 when the states vitally needed foreign aid. Despite this and despite difficulties with the British, Washington and his aides agreed that the best course for the country was strict neutrality. To the British, who ruled the seas, neutrality meant no aid for France. His Majesty's government issued orders to the Royal Navy to seize as contraband ships bearing grain and other products to France. Hundreds of American ships were captured and their crews imprisoned.

Along the Canadian border, the British also were acting to protect their interests, even at the cost of violating treaties. Faced with the danger of an attack by General Wayne, the British actually invaded the United States and established a military post, Fort Miamis, on the Maumee River (near what is now Toledo, Ohio). Moreover, Lord Dorchester, governor general of Canada, made an inflammatory speech to the Indians, who came to see him to request British armed aid against the United States. He told them that soon there would be a war between the United States and Britain and that the Indians could count on British help.

These two British actions—seizure of American ships on the high seas and warlike gestures along the northern border—brought about the crisis of 1794. Many Americans and Britons thought that a second war was inevitable. In this country there was a sharp division on what to do about the impending war.

Two prominent leaders held opposing viewpoints. Alexander Hamilton, secretary of the treasury and a leader of the Federalist party, was friendly to England and favored peace at any price. The secretary of state, Thomas Jefferson, maintained a pro-French attitude. The country, too, was divided. It soon became apparent, however, that Hamilton's views were shared by President Washington, and on the first day of December, 1793, Jefferson resigned and went back to his home at Monticello.

Early in 1794 Washington decided to seek an accommodation with the British as a last chance for peace. He selected John Jay, America's ablest diplomat, to go to London. "My objects are to prevent war, if justice can be obtained," Washington wrote.

Jay, now forty-eight and the chief justice of the United States, was reluctant. "No appointment ever operated more unpleasantly upon me, but . . . to refuse it would be to desert my duty," he wrote to his wife.

On May 12, 1794, the man who had been the prime mover in shaping the treaty of peace with England some ten years before set sail for London on an almost impossible mission. Jay knew that the temper of the nation was at the boiling point; mobs in the street were howling for British blood. He also knew that the British had the naval power to enforce their rule of the sea, no matter what neutral nations thought—and that any treaty he brought home would be castigated either by the supporters of Jefferson or by those of Hamilton. No treaty could satisfy both sides.

There were factors working for peace too, however. One

was the certainty among American leaders that peace was essential for the survival and growth of the country. Another was the size of Anglo-American trade. The United States was England's largest single customer; ninety percent of American imports came from England. Thus the maintenance of trade was important to both countries. Above all else, from the English point of view the war with France was paramount, more important even than the fur trade in the Northwest Territory. The profits from furs were not worth the risk of provoking the United States to war and a possible invasion of Canada. Certainly it would be in the British interest to keep the United States neutral.

Jay, who landed in England on June 12, had the following instructions: to conclude a settlement of all points of difference between the two countries arising from the treaty of 1783, including the evacuation of the British forts in the Ohio Valley, and to press strongly for compensation for injuries suffered as a result of British seizure of American ships and goods. He was to do all this without signing anything contrary to our treaty obligations to France and he was to insist on American rights of trade with the British West Indies without interference.

He received a friendly greeting in London from William Wyndham Grenville, the British secretary of state for foreign affairs. Baron Grenville was a man of "sound sense, steady memory and a vast industry," according to one of his biographers. The desire to reach an agreement was strong on both sides, but unfortunately for the American negotiator, the British diplomat had most of the high cards. The foreign office knew the key to Jay's codes and thus the secrets of the American negotiating terms. Moreover, Hamilton, who was playing a more and more important role in American foreign policy, undercut Jay. He told the British minister in the United States that the Americans would not join with other neutral nations in standing firm for their rights on the seas. With these handicaps, Jay met with the British.

In the United States, meanwhile, General Wayne, who was an able commander despite the reckless courage that gave him his nickname, was on the march. His army advanced slowly down the Maumee River, brushing aside modest Indian defenses, until he reached the main Indian position, a fortification of trees blown down by a storm. His mounted Kentucky riflemen raced to the sides of the Indian position and raked them with rifle fire. Then Wayne's well-trained infantry advanced and overwhelmed the Indians, who fled. The Battle of Fallen Timbers on August 20, 1794, broke the back of the Indian resistance and eliminated the main Indian threat to the Ohio Valley. But the British forts remained, an irritating thorn in the flank of the United States.

Wayne advanced toward the new British Fort Miamis.

The British commander sent out a flag of truce. What are your intentions? he asked the American commander. After all, it was a time of peace between the two nations.

Wayne replied that he was fighting hostile savages.

The British commander made it plain that if his fort was attacked, he would fight. Wayne expressed polite surprise that a British fort had been erected on American territory and requested the British to withdraw. The British commander said he was under military orders and could not move without instructions from his superiors. That was up to the diplomats, he said.

Having achieved his major objective, the destruction of the Indian force, Wayne, whose tact belied his nickname, fell back. He knew that the policy of his government was peace,

and that was, as the British commander said, up to the diplomats.

In London the diplomats, after months of negotiation,
reached agreement, largely on British terms. One historian,
Samuel Flagg Bemis, has called it the price the United States
paid for peace at a crucial period of its growth. The treaty,
signed in London on November 19, 1794, included the following terms:

1. The United States agreed to pay private prewar debts
of Americans to the British.

2. Britain agreed to submit to a mixed commission American
claims for damages arising from seizure of United States ships
and goods in the war with the French.

3. Both parties agreed to submit boundary disputes at the
northeast (Maine) and northwest (Lake of the Woods) corners
of the United States to a mixed commission.

4. Britain pledged to evacuate the frontier posts by June 1,
1796 (which was done).

Jay failed to get an agreement protecting American seamen from being impressed, or forced to serve, in the British
navy. He failed to get an agreement on the principle that
Indians on each side of the Canadian boundary should not be
interfered with by the other party. He failed to get an acknowledgment of the principles of free trade on the high seas.
For these failures, Jay was bitterly reviled on his return home.

When the treaty was finally sent to the Senate for ratification, both the treaty and Jay personally had an unpleasant
time of it. The treaty was finally ratified by the Senate on
June 24, 1795, by a straight party vote, just barely receiving
the necessary two-thirds majority, with all the Federalists vot-

ing for it and all the Jeffersonian Democratic-Republicans against it.

Despite the failures and the attacks, Jay achieved a great deal. The treaty secured control of the Northwest Territory from the machinations of the British. It also established the territorial integrity of the United States and provided the peace in which it could grow.

3

The Louisiana Purchase

TWENTY YEARS AFTER THE NEGOTIATIONS that ended the Revolutionary War, Robert R. Livingston, the new American minister to France, arrived in Paris on a delicate mission. At noon on December 6, 1801, he called to present his credentials at the Tuileries, once the palace of the kings of France and now the seat of the revolutionary government of France. As he waited, he looked out, from an upstairs window, on the courtyard below, where Napoléon Bonaparte, first consul of France, resplendent in a red coat embroidered with gold thread, sat on a splendid all-white horse, reviewing the troops of his Guard.

It was indeed a world turned upside down that Livingston found himself in. Britain, after losing her American colonies, had founded new ones and prospered. The United States had survived a peaceful transition of power from the Federalist party to the more radical Democratic-Republican party headed by Thomas Jefferson. And in France, only now was order emerging from the chaos and bloodletting that had resulted from the French Revolution. In less than two years, Bonaparte, the Corsican-born general, had extricated himself from a military debacle in Egypt and had seized firm control of the French government. His title was first consul (there were two other consuls, neither of any importance), and there was no disputing his power or his ambition.

Promptly at two P.M. Livingston presented himself in the Hall of Ministers, crowded with people of every rank, all with important business to transact with the French leader. Livingston's immediate business was merely to meet Bonaparte, a diplomatic courtesy; his real mission would come later. For almost an hour Livingston waited as servants glided through the room, serving coffee, chocolate, and liqueurs. Finally a French official escorted him through long corridors lined with Guards to an inner reception room, where Bonaparte and his closest aides received important visitors.

Bonaparte, at thirty-two the youngest man in the room, dominated it. His control over the French army and the French government was complete. He had led the army to victory over the Austrians at Marengo on June 14, 1800, which had resulted in a peace treaty that established the French border on the left bank of the Rhine. Only two months before, he had reached an agreement with the British ending the war that had started in 1793. Thus it was in a rare interval of peace that Livingston arrived.

Livingston's mission was concerned with the western and southern boundaries of the United States. At that time the United States extended only as far west as the Mississippi; across the wide Mississippi were territories owned by Spain. The southern border of the United States was the thirty-first parallel of latitude; the colonies of East Florida and West Florida to the south were also owned by Spain. One historian described the geographical situation as follows:

From the mouth of the St. Mary's, southward and westward, the shores of Florida, Louisiana and Texas were Spanish; Pensacola, Mobile and New Orleans closed all the rivers by which the United States could reach the Gulf. The Valley of the Ohio itself, as far as Pittsburgh, was at the mercy of the King of Spain; the flour and tobacco that floated down the Mississippi, or any of the rivers that fell into the Gulf, passed under the Spanish flag, and could reach a market only by permission of Don Carlos IV. Along an imaginary line from Fernandina to Natchez, some six hundred miles, and thence northward on the westward bank of the Mississippi River to the Lake of the Woods, some fourteen hundred miles farther, Spanish authority barred the path of American ambition. Of all the foreign powers, Spain alone stood in such a position as to make violence sooner or later inevitable even to the pacific Jefferson.

The key to this enormous area was the seaport city of New Orleans, on the eastern bank of the Mississippi, south of the thirty-first parallel. In those days before roads and rails, the most economical means to ship goods was by boat and barge. A farmer in western Pennsylvania, for example, found it easier and cheaper to send his produce down the Ohio and the Mississippi to the Gulf of Mexico and then by ship to Philadelphia than to send it overland by the rough mountain trails.

This fact of economic geography was quite clear to all American diplomats, and in every treaty they had successfully included articles providing for freedom of shipment down the Mississippi. In the Pinckney Treaty of 1795, for example, Spain gave citizens of the United States the right to navigate the waters of the Mississippi River and to deposit their goods at New Orleans for transshipment without paying taxes.

The United States was not content with this situation. There would be no problem as long as Spain, an impotent power, controlled these regions. What caused concern was that, as almost all Americans knew, the colonies still held by European countries in America were pawns in the hands of imperial powers; they could change ownership at any time, in war or peace, as it suited these powers. Rumors that Spain had ceded Louisiana back to the French were causing great alarm in the United States. President Jefferson knew that one spot on the globe could not be possessed by France if United States interests were to prosper. He wrote:

> It is New Orleans, through which the produce of three-eighths of our territory must pass to market, and from its fertility, it will ere long yield more than half our whole produce, and contain more than half of our inhabitants. France, placing herself in that door, assumes to us the attitude of defiance. Spain might have retained it quietly for years.

Unknown to the Americans, the retrocession of Louisiana (which included New Orleans) had already been decided. The king of Spain and Bonaparte had agreed to the Treaty of San Ildefonso in 1800, calling for the return of Louisiana to France. In that treaty, Napoléon created a kingdom in Tuscany for the son-in-law of the king and queen of Spain; in return, Napoléon demanded and received the vast Louisiana territory, which France had given to Spain in 1762 to keep it from the British.

It was part of Livingston's mission, in fact, to find out if the rumored retrocession had taken place. His instructions also included the following: if the cession was irrevocable, to make sure that our rights of navigation of the Mississippi were safeguarded; to find out if the Floridas were included and, if they were, to convince France to yield them, or at least West Florida, to the United States; and lastly, if the rumors were not well founded, to induce France to help the United States obtain the region from Spain.

It was with these delicate considerations in mind that Livingston, the fifty-five-year-old Hudson River aristocrat, faced Bonaparte, the ambitious soldier. Livingston, who had been quite friendly to the French during the revolutionary period in the United States, read French well, but he spoke it poorly, and in addition he had hearing problems. Diplomatic niceties, then, were exchanged through an interpreter.

Have you been in Europe before? Bonaparte asked.

No.

You have come to a very corrupt world, Bonaparte said.

The description was accurate. The world of the French court was indeed corrupt. It was beginning to take on some of the characteristics of the monarchy that had been forcibly deposed only twelve years before. Bribery was common, fidelity rare. The name of one man in that room during the short exchange has come down to personify corruption in government, and it was quite clear that Bonaparte was alluding to him, Charles-Maurice de Talleyrand-Périgord, the French foreign minister. And it was with Talleyrand that Livingston would have to conduct his business, although no one doubted that Bonaparte himself would make all the major decisions.

Thus, on a keynote that scarcely kindled any hope for Livingston's mission, began more than a year and a half of negotiation. Contrary to what most history books relate, Livingston's purpose was not to purchase Louisiana. His mission was much more limited: to secure peaceful rights for Americans on the Mississippi River and in the port of New Orleans. The right of Americans to transship their merchandise in New Orleans, vital as it was to the United States, was an unimportant detail to the French. More important to

Bonaparte was the grandeur of France, and even more important than that was his own ambition.

Bonaparte's imperial design seemed quite clear. He had moved toward French conquest of the routes to India with the expedition to Egypt in 1799; it had failed. Now with title to Louisiana (although the French would not admit the fact to the Americans), and to the island of Haiti in the Caribbean, he could weld a Caribbean empire of vast riches—if he could take possession of Haiti, racked by a revolt of the natives, and if he could occupy Louisiana and the Floridas. Spain was unimportant in this design; the United States, a trifle. But England, stubborn England and its navy, stood in Napoléon's way.

In this hotbed of intrigue, Livingston found himself and his project mostly ignored. Talleyrand misled him and lied to him. The French would not admit that the Treaty of San Ildefonso had been signed, which it had been; and here was Livingston trying to convince the French that the treaty was not in France's interests. Livingston was trying to buy West Florida from France by assuming payment of private claims against the French. But West Florida had not been ceded to France by Spain, and the French did not recognize the debts. It was a curious venture for Livingston, who was finding, as had Jay and Adams before him, that the Americans and the United States were, at best, a piece on the chessboard of imperial rivalries.

Doggedly, the American envoy made the diplomatic rounds. He had two French friends, the marquis de Lafayette and François de Barbé-Marbois, the French minister of finance, who had been French minister to the United States at the time of the negotiations that ended the Revolutionary War, when Livingston had been secretary for foreign affairs.

The year 1802 was one of maneuver. The French made efforts to subdue Haiti. The French and the British formally signed the Peace of Amiens, ending their most recent conflict, and the French immediately began to plan a new war. In Washington, President Jefferson, hardening his position against French possessions, put out tentative feelers for the purchase of the Floridas. In Paris, Livingston was making no progress in his mission.

The island of Haiti was controlled by Toussaint-L'Ouverture, the rebellious black leader, and a half million former slaves. An expedition under the command of General Charles Leclerc, husband of Bonaparte's sister Pauline, was sent to put down the rebellion. At that same time Bonaparte sent a letter to Toussaint expressing friendship. "We take pleasure in recognizing and proclaiming the great services you have rendered to the French people," Bonaparte wrote. The French expedition landed in January and suffered a disastrous defeat. But after treachery on the Haitian side, Toussaint surrendered and was sent back to France, prison, and death.

With Haiti apparently in his possession, Bonaparte tried to obtain the Floridas from Spain, but the Spanish delayed. The British also delayed in surrendering Malta to the French, as required by the Treaty of Amiens. The French, too, delayed; they were not interested in talking to Livingston, who wanted to clarify the French position in America.

Jefferson wrote to Livingston, rejecting a proposal to solve the problem by granting Americans free access to the sea. The United States had a natural friendship for France, he stated, but the national characteristics of the two peoples were so divergent that they could not live side by side peacefully for any length of time. Even the cession by France of the Floridas and New Orleans would only delay, but not suppress, unavoidable conflict. The only acceptable solution was for

France to give up the rights she had acquired under the Treaty of San Ildefonso.

Jefferson also wrote:

> The day that France takes possession of New Orleans, fixes the sentence which is to restrain her for ever within her low water mark. It seals the union of two nations, who, in conjunction, can maintain exclusive possession of the ocean. From that day forward, we must marry ourselves to the British fleet and nation. We must turn our attention to a maritime force, for which our resources place us on a very high ground; and having formed and connected together a power which may render reinforcements of her settlements here impossible to France, make the first cannon fired in Europe the signal for the tearing up of any settlement she may have made, and for holding of the two continents of America in sequestration for the common purposes of the United British and American nations. This is not a state of things we seek or desire.

In Paris, Livingston prepared an analysis of the question "Is it advantageous to France to take possession of Louisiana?" His arguments were that it would not help French commerce or manufacturing and that, in truth, it would weaken the French. If France were to cede New Orleans to the United States, he went on, France could have all the advantages of trade there without the expense of maintaining it and would keep on friendly terms with the United States.

While this message was being translated and circulated, James Madison, the American secretary of state, wrote to Livingston pointing out what was obvious to all, that the mere proximity of France would be harmful to relations between the two countries. He went further. He asked Livingston to find out the price of New Orleans and the Floridas. Livingston replied that they would be cheap at $20 million, the first time a specific figure had been mentioned even in idle talk about a purchase.

Inside France, Bonaparte moved step by step toward the realization of his own ambition. On August 4, 1802, a plebiscite overwhelmingly adopted a new constitution that made him consul for life, with the right to name his own successor— only a step away from a throne. Livingston commented in a letter to Madison: "There never was a government in which less could be done by negotiation than here. There is no people, no legislature, no concillors. One man is everything. He seldom asks advice and never hears it unasked—his ministers are clerks and his legislature and concillors parade officers."

In the United States, the Louisiana issue was ready to explode. In October 1802 the Spanish governor of New Orleans closed the port to Americans. American merchandise thenceforth could not be deposited in New Orleans for shipment to the East Coast or abroad; thus was American trade in the Mississippi Valley effectively halted. The action was taken in reprisal against American smuggling and had no connection, apparently, with the imperial chess game going on in Europe.

It caused an uproar in the United States and brought threats of war by western interests. These moves were reflected in Congress, which demanded to know what was going on. On December 17 Jefferson replied that he was "aware of the obligation to maintain in all cases the rights of the nation, and to employ for that purpose, those just and honorable means which belong to the character of the United States." This was a polite way of saying that he was considering the use of force.

The importance of New Orleans to United States trade was indicated by a report from a French observer there: "In front of the city and along the quays there are at this moment fifty-five American ships to ten French. . . . If New Orleans has been peopled and acquired importance and capital, it is due neither to Spain or to the Louisianans. . . . It is due to three hundred thousand planters who in twenty years have swarmed across the eastern plains of the Mississippi and have cultivated them and have no other outlet than this river and no other port than New Orleans."

Livingston, who had been conducting private talks with Joseph Bonaparte, brother of the first consul, said flatly that the United States would never permit the Mississippi to be closed. If Spain did not open the port of New Orleans, the United States certainly would be forced to take action. This would mean a closer association with Britain, something that surely would not be in the interests of France. Upon hearing these ominous words, which sounded like war, Joseph Bonaparte, who had been chatting about minor matters, hastily retreated from his role as intermediary.

On January 10, 1803, Livingston wrote to Talleyrand, saying that Louisiana without the Floridas was useless to France; that the United States should possess all of Louisiana above the Arkansas River, since this would place a barrier of Americans between British Canada and French Louisiana; that France should own East Florida as far as the Perdido River but should cede New Orleans and West Florida to the United States.

On the following day in Washington, President Jefferson, who of course knew nothing of Livingston's initiative, sent a message to the Senate recommending that James Monroe of Virginia be sent to Paris with full powers jointly with Livingston to enter into a treaty with France for "the purpose of enlarging and more effectively securing our rights and interests on the River Mississippi and in the territories eastward thereof."

The instructions of Monroe and Livingston, dated March 2,

1803, gave the American objective in further detail: "to procure by just and satisfactory arrangements a cession to the United States of New Orleans and of West and East Florida, or as much thereof as the actual proprietor can be prevailed to part with." The price was not to go above $9,375,000. It was made pointedly clear, in the attached draft of a proposed treaty, that France could reserve to herself all the territory on the west side of the Mississippi River. Thus once again it was made explicit that the United States concern lay with New Orleans, not with expansion of her borders across the Mississippi.

These first months of 1803 were a time of crisis for Bonaparte too. On January 7 he learned that his brother-in-law, General Leclerc, had died in Haiti and that his army there had been decimated by guerrilla warfare and yellow fever. Another French expedition to Haiti was frozen into Dutch ports and unable to leave until the ice melted. The Spanish were being obstinate about yielding Florida. The Americans, as noted by Bonaparte's ambassador to Washington, were growing more belligerent about their rights on the Mississippi. Bonaparte began to lose interest in his dream of a Caribbean empire.

Monroe reached Le Havre on April 8, and two days later Livingston received a letter announcing his arrival. Also on April 10, Napoléon met with Barbé-Marbois, his finance minister, and Denis Decrés, minister of marine. They talked of the impending war with Britain, and Bonaparte mentioned that Britain would certainly seize Louisiana.

"I think of ceding it to the United States," he said. He also noted that it was not yet even in French possession.

"They ask of me only one town in Louisiana," he said, "but I already consider the colony as entirely lost, and it appears to me that in the hands of this growing power it will be more useful to the policy and even the commerce of France than if I should attempt to keep it."

On April 11 Bonaparte once again summoned Barbé-Marbois and said: "I renounce Louisiana."

"It is not only New Orleans that I cede," he went on, "it is the whole colony without reserve. I know the price of what I abandon. I have proved the importance I attach to this province, since my first diplomatic act with Spain had the object of recovering it. I renounce it with great regret; to attempt obstinately to retain it would be folly."

He then directed Barbé-Marbois to settle the matter. "Do not even wait for the arrival of Mr. Monroe; have an interview this very day with Mr. Livingston."

On that fateful April 11, Talleyrand asked Livingston to call and quite unexpectedly and blandly asked if the United States wanted the whole of Louisiana. Livingston was stunned. This was much more than the United States had asked for, more than it hoped for. But he replied, no, American wishes extended only to New Orleans and the Floridas.

Talleyrand persisted. If we give New Orleans, the rest of Louisiana is of little value, he said. What would the United States give for it all?

Livingston said perhaps $3,750,000.

That was too low, Talleyrand said.

Two days later the conversation was resumed, but this time between Livingston and Barbé-Marbois. The Frenchman related that Napoléon had set the price for Louisiana at $22,500,000, part of this being the American assumption of claims against France. This was a huge sum in those days, but it was a bargain by any standard.

Livingston approached the transaction like a horse trader. He repeated that the United States really had no interest in the west bank of the Mississippi. Moreover, he said the price was exorbitant. After a lengthy conversation, Barbé-Marbois finally said he would accept somewhat less. Livingston said it was still too much.

When the talks broke off near midnight, Livingston hastily wrote to Madison:

> The field opened to us is infinitely larger than our instructions contemplate, the revenues increasing and the lands more than adequate to sink the capital should we ever go to the length proposed by Barbé-Marbois. Nay I persuade myself that the whole sum may be raised by the sale of the territory west of the Mississippi with the right of sovereignty to some power in Europe whose vicinity we should not fear. . . . We shall do all we can to cheapen the purchase but my present sentiment is that we shall buy.

The bargaining proceeded. Livingston made an offer; Barbé-Marbois insisted he would take no less than $11,250,000 for Louisiana and $3,750,000 more for the claims. The Americans agreed, apparently for the first time grasping the tremendous nature of the purchase, and asked for a speedy completion of the deal.

On May 2 Livingston and Monroe signed the treaty for the United States, and Barbé-Marbois for France. Livingston said: "We have lived long, but this is the noblest work of our whole lives. . . . From this day forward, the United States takes its place among the powers of the first rank." Napoléon said: "This accession of territory affirms forever the power of the United States, and I have just given England a maritime rival that sooner or later will lay low her pride."

The Louisiana Purchase raised questions about six major points:

1. Bonaparte sold Louisiana before the retrocession by Spain was completed; thus, to some, it was not even his to sell.

2. The Treaty of San Ildefonso contained a clause providing that if there was any attempt to cede Louisiana to a third party, it would revert back to Spain.

3. Bonaparte sold the territory without consulting the French Senate or Legislative Assembly, so that the sale was unconstitutional according to French law. (But there was no one in France in a position to dispute the first consul.)

4. There was doubt whether the transaction was valid according to the United States Constitution. Even Jefferson at one time had said: "The Constitution has made no provisions for our holding foreign territory."

5. It was not certain whether West Florida was included.

6. The exact boundaries of Louisiana were not defined. It was impossible to be precise either about the boundaries or about the total area involved. Measurements much later gave 831,321 square miles as the extent of the Louisiana Purchase, slightly less than the 891,364 square miles that made up the entire United States before the purchase.

The first three of these points, mainly concerned with French and Spanish rights, were generally ignored. The last three were important in the United States, however, and a great debate ensued.

The *Trenton Federalist* summarized the views of the opposition: "What will it be but a drain for the money and men of our country, ruinous to our agriculture, commerce and manufacturing?" Describing the purchase as "a scheme which promises no good, but much evil to the United States," the paper went on: "If this country is so important to the Western people, let them pay for it themselves." Careful note was

A view of New Orleans in 1803. The American eagle in the sky signifies the United States, of which New Orleans is now a part. *Chicago Historical Society.*

made of the fact that the Constitution made no provision for the purchase of additional lands.

But the opposition, however vocal, was really minor. Most Americans viewed the prospect of doubling the area of their country as a glorious feat; the size of the acquisition dwarfed the constitutional question, even for Jefferson. On October 20, 1803, the Senate ratified the treaty of purchase by a vote of twenty-four to seven.

What did Louisiana actually encompass? No one really knew. A French document, written just before the purchase, described it as follows:

> The colony of Louisiana is a vast province located west of the Mississippi, which forms on that side its common boundary with the United States.
>
> On the west, it is bounded by New Mexico, on the south by

the sea, and at the north by a limitless extent of lands scarcely known. . . .

The extent of Louisiana, the boundary of which has only been indicated above, is well determined at the south by the Gulf of Mexico. . . .

The farther north one goes, the more indecisive becomes the boundary.

That part of America scarcely includes more than uninhabited forests or Indian tribes, and hitherto no necessity has been felt of establishing a line of demarcation.

Neither does any boundary exist between Louisiana and Canada.

The French and the Spanish clearly understood, however, that the part of Louisiana that was purchased on the east bank of the Mississippi included only the city of New Orleans, no more. The remainder of the lands east of the Mississippi and south of the thirty-first parallel, the southern boundary of the United States, belonged to West and East Florida, colonies of Spain. The Americans, who at first agreed with this definition, gradually began to enlarge it to make claims to West Florida.

While the diplomats tried to make definite lines out of vague boundary lines, the United States moved swiftly to take possession of Louisiana. The French, however, could not yield it until they themselves had taken possession from Spain. On November 30, 1803, Pierre Clement Laussat, the French commissioner, formally received the colony from Spanish officials.

Twenty days later, at noon on December 20, the French, in turn, surrendered Louisiana to the Americans in a ceremony in New Orleans. French soldiers slowly lowered the tricolor, and an officer silently folded it and carried it to the rear. American soldiers than started to raise their flag, but the ropes on the flagpole stuck, as one spectator wrote, "as if it were confused at taking the place of that to which it owed its glorious independence."

An anxious silence reigned, according to this eyewitness, among the crowds in the plaza, and it was not until the flag reached the top that loud cries of "huzzah" burst forth from a small group of Americans, who waved their hats in joy. These cries made even more gloomy the silence of the French and Spanish spectators, some of whom were moved to tears.

"The Standard of my country was, this day, unfurled here, amidst the reiterated acclamations of thousands." William C. C. Claiborne, the new American governor, wrote to James Madison, the secretary of state. "And if I may judge by profession and appearances, the Government of the United States is received with joy and gratitude by the people."

Thus was completed the transfer of lower Louisiana to the Americans, but upper Louisiana still remained in Spanish possession. It was an absurd technicality, but the transfer of the enormous tract would not be official until the ceremonies were completed. Laussat asked the American officer chosen to accept the area for the United States if he would first accept the land in the name of France. So it was that Amos Stoddard, a captain in the United States Corps of Artillery, became a commissioner for a day for France.

On March 9, 1804, a small group of United States soldiers commanded by Captain Stoddard marched up the slope leading from the banks of the Mississippi River to the rough wooden building that was the capital of upper Louisiana. As drums beat and cannons fired a salute, the flag of Spain was lowered and the French flag was raised. Captain Stoddard accepted the province in the name of France.

On March 10 a similar ceremony took place. At that second ceremony the flag of France was lowered and the Stars and Stripes was raised in its place. Stoddard, the commissioner for France, turned the vast territory of the upper Mississippi Valley over to Stoddard, the commissioner for the United States. He spoke to the few residents of the area, mostly French:

> You now form an integral part of a great community, the powers of whose government are circumscribed and defined by charter. . . . You may soon expect the establishment of a territorial government. . . . From your present population, and the rapidity of its increase, this territorial establishment must soon be succeeded by your admission as a state into the Federal Union.

It was not until fifteen years later that the United States knew the actual boundaries of the lands it had acquired. Fifteen years of diplomacy resulted in the Adams–de Onís Treaty (John Quincy Adams for the United States and Luis de Onís for Spain), giving these boundaries to the Louisiana Purchase:

> The boundary line between the two countries, west of the Mississippi, shall begin on the Gulf of Mexico, at the mouth of the River Sabine, in the sea; continuing north, along the western bank of that river, to the thirty-second degree of latitude; thence on a line due north to the degree of latitude where it strikes the Rio Roxo of Nachitoches, or Red River; then following the course of the Rio Roxo westward, to the degree of longitude one hundred west from London and twenty-three from Washington; then, crossing the said Red River, and running thence, by a line due north to the River Arkansas; thence following the course of the southern bank of the Arkansas, to its source in latitude forty-two degrees north, and thence by that parallel of latitude to the South sea.

4

Florida

THE INDIANS OF THE CARIBBEAN knew of a fabulous island, Bimini, filled with everything a person could desire—gold, delicious fruit, and—more exciting to the Spanish explorers of the sixteenth century—a marvelous spring of water that had the magical power of making old people young again. Juan Ponce de León, who had come to the New World on Columbus's second voyage in 1493, listened carefully to these tales. He was almost fifty, rich from the gold, land, and slaves he had found in his conquest of Puerto Rico. It became his ambition to find Bimini and that wonderful fountain of youth.

In 1513, bearing a commission from King Ferdinand of Spain, he set out in three ships to find a treasure that would be greater than all the gold, silver, and jewels his fellow explorers were taking back to Spain. He discovered some small islands, none of which had any fountains at all. Then on April 2, 1513, he set foot on a new land, which he called La Florida because it was Easter Sunday (Pascua Florida, in Spanish). He landed at a point 175 miles south of what is now St. Augustine, and then sailed down the coast, past the Miami area and the Keys. He saw Indians, but there was no sign of the magical springs of Bimini.

Reluctantly Ponce de León started back for Puerto Rico and Spain, where he related his adventures to the king. In September 1514 the king commissioned Ponce to settle "the isle of Bimini," which he had not yet discovered, and "the isle of Florida," which he had. Before doing so, he was ordered to lead an expedition to subdue the Indians on the islands of the Caribbean south of Puerto Rico.

He wrote to the king: "I discovered at my own cost and charge the island Florida and others in its district and now I return to that island, if it please God's will, to settle it and I also intend to explore the coast of said island further, and see whether it is an island." But it was not until 1521 that Ponce was able to set out once again for Florida. He loaded two hundred men and fifty horses, as well as domestic animals and farm equipment, in two ships and sailed westward.

On this, his second trip to Florida, Ponce de León landed on the west coast, possibly near what is now Tampa Bay. Hostile Indians greeted him and his men with a shower of arrows. Ponce was wounded so severely that his flagship immediately set sail for Cuba, and there he died several days later, at the age of sixty-one.

Other Spanish explorers followed Ponce de León in pursuing phantom goals of quick riches of gold and jewels in the Americas. Many of them used Florida as a base for their operations, which took them across the southern United States and into Mexico and Central and South America. One of these men was Hernando de Soto, who had served under Francisco Pizarro in the conquest of Peru. He obtained from the king of Spain a contract to conquer Florida and, with an army of seven hundred men, landed, on May 30, 1539, near Tampa Bay. Thus began a three-year odyssey in quest of gold and riches that was to produce death and disease—and discovery.

De Soto marched his army through what is now Florida, Georgia, North and South Carolina, Tennessee, Alabama, Mississippi, Arkansas, Oklahoma, and Texas (and detachments may even have entered Missouri and Louisiana). Behind them, the Spaniards left a trail of butchery. Indians shot at them from the protection of trees. Indian guides who tried to mislead the marching army were torn to shreds by bloodhounds, and Indians who refused to talk were also thrown to the savage dogs. Indian villages were pillaged and burned. Almost everywhere, the Indians, anxious to speed the ravaging Spaniards out of their lands, told them stories of gold just a few days farther on. The invaders found nothing but cold and starvation—and more hostile Indians.

In May 1541 the ragged remnants of de Soto's army, barefoot and emaciated, foundered through the swamps of western Mississippi. They traveled slowly, for many were wounded; most had no hope. At last they found themselves in front of a broad river, the widest they had ever seen. They called it the Rio Grande, the big river. Without knowing it, they had discovered the Mississippi River. But all they knew was that it was wide and swift, difficult to cross, and that there were more Indians on the other side.

They managed to cross the broad Mississippi and then wandered northward, still seeking the riches that other Spanish explorers had discovered in Mexico and Peru. They wintered in Arkansas and crossed back into Mississippi. Somewhere along the lower Mississippi River, discouraged and diseased, de Soto died, not knowing that he had made a major geographical discovery. His body was buried, disinterred, and then ceremoniously consigned to the river, so that his Indian enemies could not find it and dishonor him. In 1543 the remainder of the army built some rude boats and fought its way downstream to the Gulf of Mexico and thence to the Mexican coast.

For more than two hundred years Spain retained control of Florida, which included all of Spanish North America east of the Mississippi. French explorers came down the Mississippi from the St. Lawrence and the Great Lakes (La Salle in 1682). France claimed, in the name of Louis XIV, all the lands drained by the Mississippi and called the area Louisiana.

British colonizers at first came only as far south as Charleston, South Carolina, but by 1743 the British reached the St. Mary's River (which is part of the present boundary between Georgia and Florida). Just before the French conceded defeat and the end of their aspirations in North America, they transferred Louisiana to Spain to keep it from falling into the hands of the British. But in the Treaty of Peace of 1763, by which France yielded to England all her North American possessions (except Louisiana), the British insisted that Spain, France's ally, give up Florida.

Thus began twenty years of British rule in Florida. First the area was divided at the Apalachicola River into two provinces, East and West Florida. The original northern boundary of the region was the thirty-first degree of north latitude, but the boundary of West Florida was now advanced northward to 32°20' to encourage settlement along the Mississippi. Settlers did come; they built houses and they fostered trade, mostly in furs, but it was too late. The American Revolution was beginning—and the British had three enemies to face: the Americans, the French, and the Spanish.

An energetic Spaniard, Bernardo de Gálvez, went off to fight the British as soon as he learned that his country had declared war in 1779. Up from New Orleans, Gálvez's small army marched—170 Spanish veterans, 300 recruits from the Canary Islands, 20 musketeers, 60 militiamen, 80 free blacks and mulattoes, and one American, Oliver Pollock. As they moved up to the river, they were joined by hundreds of farmers, trappers, and Indians. They marched through the forests to reach Manchac, the British town 115 miles above New Orleans.

On September 6 the Spanish attacked the poorly defended British fort guarding Manchac and captured it without suffering any casualties. Then the army marched north to Baton Rouge, which defended itself more strongly, but after an artillery battle it too surrendered. Gálvez captured Natchez and then swiftly moved east, taking Mobile and Pensacola without much trouble. The Spanish recaptured East and West Florida, and in 1783, in the peace treaty that ended the American Revolution, they regained formal possession of the Floridas.

Glance at a map of Florida at the time of the Louisiana Purchase—it looks like a gun held against New Orleans. East Florida is the handle and West Florida the barrel. Americans viewed Spanish possession of the Floridas as a threat against the United States. The United States could never be secure with Spain sitting on its southern doorstep. Though Spain was a weak power, one day it might turn Florida over to a stronger power, England or France, just as other colonial possessions had been transferred in the past. In Paris in 1803, Livingston had tried to purchase Florida, as well as New Orleans; he had failed in his bid for Florida, despite the great bargain he had gained for his country in the vast Louisiana Purchase.

Now, in 1804, two major boundary questions confronted the United States in the south: the boundaries of Florida and the limits of the Louisiana Purchase. For fifteen years American diplomacy was to grapple with these two problems, which were tied together by the fact that the American adversary was Spain, even though the two areas were geographically separated.

On the land itself, on the beautiful and fertile land of West Florida, with its magnificent hickory and oak forests, men of many nationalities built farms and set up trading posts, and competed for control. The Spanish were the official owners; but the new Americans, many of them fugitives from justice, flocked in to earn a living, and made orderly government all but impossible. There were Frenchmen, Englishmen, Tories, and even pirates, many of them men who drank, fought, and argued hard.

Among the disputatious settlers were three giant brothers, Reuben Kemper, six feet six, and Nathan and Sam, only a little shorter. They settled along the Mississippi just north of Baton Rouge in an area of rolling hills and grassy prairies. Before long, Nathan got into an argument with the Spanish agent and was ordered off the land. He refused to go. The Spanish governor sent a small gunboat and the Kemper boys retreated. They held a council of war, decided that West Florida should be free, and commissioned a declaration of independence, which read:

> For a people to be free it is sufficient that they will it. Whereas the despotism under which we have long groaned has grown into an insupportable burden, and as it is long admitted that men are born with equal rights, we the undersigned inhabitants of the dominion called West Florida, have resolved to throw off the galling yoke of tyranny and become free men, by declaring ourselves a free and independent people, and by supporting with our lives and property this declaration.

They designed a flag—two white stars and seven alternating blue and white stripes—and banding together an army of thirty men, they invaded Spanish territory on August 7, 1804. Unfortunately for them, no residents of West Florida joined their colors, and they were routed when the Spanish militia blocked the road to Baton Rouge. Thus ended the first attempt to free West Florida from Spanish rule.

As the country grew, so too grew the American population and the desire for independence. This came to a head in 1810 when rumors circulated that Napoléon Bonaparte was about to seize Florida. The Americans in the area disliked the Spanish, but they hated and feared Bonaparte and the French. On June 23, 1810, more than five hundred residents met north of Baton Rouge and declared their allegiance to Spain and their opposition to France. They also nominated officials for a local government, something they had not had before.

Even though this convention declared its support of Spain, the local governor determined to suppress the growing independence movement. But the settlers struck first. On September 21, 1810, the Bayou Sara Horse, a company of local dragoons twenty-one strong, started out for Baton Rouge. By midnight, grown to about seventy-five men, they arrived at the outskirts of Baton Rouge, which was protected by a Spanish fort amply garrisoned with troops and artillery. There was absolutely no chance to storm the fort.

One backwoodsman observed that the cows of the garrison were led out every morning on the foggy riverside and then were brought back at milking time. If the cows could come and go, so could horsemen. At dawn the next morning, in a thick fog, mounted men mingled with the cows on the cowpath near the river.

"Who is there?" a sentry shouted.

There was no answer.

"Who goes there?" the sentry demanded.

Again no answer.

"Alert, alert!" shouted the sentry, and sleepy Spanish soldiers tumbled out of their barracks.

"Fire!" ordered the Spanish commander. The soldiers fired at the Americans, but no one was hit.

The Americans fired back, wounding the Spanish commander and many of his soldiers. In a moment the battle was over. The Spanish surrendered.

Before the sun was full in the sky, the Americans pulled down the red-and-yellow flag of Spain and raised in its stead a blue flag with a white star that had been made by the wife of Major Isaac Johnson. The major then tied the Spanish flag to his horse's tail and rode through the streets of Baton Rouge, followed by his cavalrymen shouting that a new republic had just been born. On September 26, 1810, the West Floridians declared their independence of Spain, proclaimed the Republic of West Florida, and sent a commissioner to the United States to seek annexation and a loan.

While these events were occurring in Florida, the policy of the United States was taking shape, once again being forged in the European rivalries of Spain, France, and England. Bonaparte had conquered Spain in 1808; he was again at war with Britain; and again the threat of a British army fighting on the southern borders of the United States was real. The government in Washington felt that the British might intervene, not only in Florida, but in the rebellious Spanish colonies of Central and South America. On October 27 the West Floridians' request for annexation was met by a proclamation by President Madison that West Florida was actually part of Louisiana and had been all along. He directed Governor Claiborne of Louisiana to take possession of West Florida as far east as the Perdido River.

Claiborne came into Baton Rouge accompanied by five gunboats and American troops. The Florida rebels were indignant at what they considered highhanded behavior on the part of the United States. The first time Claiborne raised the American flag over Baton Rouge, it was torn down. But annexation to the United States was what the rebels really wanted, and they gave up. Seventy-four days after the formation of the government of West Florida, the territory disappeared into the vastness of the United States. The Spanish, however, maintained that they still had legal ownership of West Florida—and they held physical and legal possession of East Florida.

One of the major reasons the West Floridians had for supporting annexation was fear of Britain. The British had not given up their territorial ambitions in the Caribbean; indeed, they retained their colonies in the West Indies and sent agents into East Florida to stir up the Indians. In the fading Spanish empire, there was opportunity for trade and for trouble. To make matters even more complex, Britain was still at war with the French, which caused the British to impress American seamen in the Atlantic and violate the rights of neutrals—actions much resented by the United States. This, combined with an American expansionist movement in the south and west, led to the War of 1812.

The Floridas were one of the key areas in the war. Even before war broke out, the northern part of East Florida, the region around the St. Mary's River, was the scene of intrigue by American, Spanish, British, Indian, and independent adventurers. Along these borders British ships regularly smuggled goods into the United States; Spanish authority was weak. Into this vacuum advanced a band of two hundred men. They met at St. Mary's in March 1812, established a republican government, and hoisted their own flag—a white field with an armed soldier on it, bearing the motto: The Safety of the People—the Supreme Law.

From his home in the Hermitage, just outside Nashville,

Major General Andrew Jackson issued the following plea that same March, a few months before the actual declaration of war against England.

VOLUNTEERS TO ARMS

Citizens!
A simple invitation is given for 50,000 volunteers. Shall we, who have clamored for war, now skulk into a corner? Are we titled Slaves of George the third? the military conscripts of Napoléon? or the frozen peasants of the Russian Czar? No— we are the free born sons of the only republick now existing in the world.

Men of the West flocked to the colors, but no orders for them came from Washington. Jackson trained and took care of his troops; he visited the sick, made sure they were fed; on foot, he tirelessly made the rounds, supervising the men in the ranks. "He's tough," one of the soldiers commented. "Tough as hickory," another said. Before long, the soldiers added an affectionate adjective, and Jackson became "Old Hickory."

His first military venture was not against the British; it was against Indians. The Creek had revolted in the Mississippi territory (in what is now the state of Alabama), and Jackson and his men were sent to subdue them. It took until March 1814 to put down the Indians. During all this fighting, Jackson kept his eyes on Florida, where British agents, soldiers, and ships were preparing for an invasion of the United States.

Other battles of the War of 1812 were fought along the Maine-Canada border, along the Great Lakes, and along the Eastern seaboard, and there were important events in the south as well. Jackson, commanding the Third United States Infantry, 535 men strong, moved south into Mobile on August 22, 1814, just two days before the British captured and burned Washington, D.C. A British fleet was at anchor at Pensacola; the British had a marine garrison at Fort Barrancas. The British commander had issued the following proclamation:

Natives of Louisiana; on you the first call is made to Assist in Liberating your paternal soil. American Usurpation must be Abolished. I am at the head of a large body of Indians, well-armed, disciplined and commanded by British officers—a good train of artillery, seconded by numerous British and Spanish squadron. Be not alarmed at our approach. A flag over any door, whether Spanish, British or French, will be certain Protection.

The British intention was clear. It was to capture New Orleans, the key to the Mississippi River and to the Gulf of Mexico.

On September 3, 1814, the British brig *Sophie* slowly approached the Louisiana coast near Lake Barataria, south of New Orleans. Two English officers landed from a small boat and approached a crowd of barefoot seamen.

"Monsieur Laffite?" one of the officers asked.

"Messieurs, I myself am Laffite," one of the seamen, a tall, sunburned man, said. His voice was mild, his manner pleasant. He invited the British officers for dinner; they drank a good wine and lighted fragrant cigars.

The Louisiana host was the gentleman pirate Laffite, the king of Lake Barataria. His ships combed the Gulf of Mexico for Spanish vessels and after taking them would offer their cargoes for sale in New Orleans; he owned a warehouse on Royal Street. Governor Claiborne had offered a reward of $750 for the capture of Laffite. The pirate, in turn, had offered $1,500 for the capture of Claiborne. Jean Laffite was perfectly safe in the bayous around Barataria.

The British officers got down to business. They offered

An illustration based on John Landis's unfinished painting "The Battle of New Orleans." *Anne S. K. Brown Military Collection, Brown University Library.*

Laffite an appointment as captain in the British service if he would help the British capture New Orleans. Laffite asked for fifteen days to consider their proposal.

Pirate though he was, Laffite was a patriot. He promptly wrote a letter to Claiborne, saying: "This point of Louisiana that I occupy is of Great Importance in the present situation. I offer myself to defend it. I am the Lost Sheep who desires to return to the flock."

Through a comedy of errors, Claiborne's officers decided that the letter was a forgery and, though the British were almost at hand, sent an expedition to destroy Barataria. Laffite fled.

Meanwhile Jackson, the American commander, believed that the British would advance on New Orleans through Mobile, where he and his small army were camped. He felt that Pensacola, farther to the east, was the key to the whole region.

"As I act without the orders of the government," Jackson wrote Secretary of State Monroe, "I deem it important to state to you my reasons. The safety of this section of the union depends on it, and Pensacola has assumed the character of British Territory."

On November 6 Jackson's three thousand men stormed Pensacola, in violation of the technical neutrality of Spain. Jackson had decided to risk being absent from Mobile and New Orleans—but he found that the British had fled from Pensacola. The British flight had an important side effect, however. It ruined their prestige among the Creek and Seminole Indians, who fled into the Florida wilderness.

Jackson hastened back to Mobile and thence to New Orleans. Meanwhile, a British fleet carrying ten thousand seamen, fifteen hundred marines and almost ten thousand soldiers, sailed toward New Orleans. They were so sure of victory that the officers' wives, with trunkloads of pretty clothes, accompanied them.

In full dress uniform, a blue frock coat with buff facings, white waistcoat, and close-fitting white breeches, Jackson arrived in New Orleans on December 1. He found the city in great alarm, fearful that the British were indeed coming and that they would succeed in capturing it.

On December 14 the British force overwhelmed an American naval guard on Lake Borgne, on the outskirts of New Orleans. But Jackson stood ready to defend New Orleans, and with him was every man of fighting age in the area, with the sole exception of the pirates of Lake Barataria.

Jean Laffite, who had been in hiding, boldly walked down Royal Street one evening and requested an audience with Jackson. No record of the conversation between the mild-mannered pirate and the quick-tempered general was made, but one of Jackson's officers later recalled:

> Mr. Laffite solicited for himself and for all Baratarians the honor of serving under our banners, that they might have an opportunity of proving that if they had infringed the revenue laws, yet none were more ready than they to defend the country. Persuaded that the assistance of these men could not fail of being very useful, the general accepted their efforts.

Artillery detachments were formed under the command of Laffite's assistant, Dominique You, who had served as an artilleryman under Bonaparte. This was accomplished just in time for the defense of New Orleans. The British made a surprise landing on the night of December 23, just below the city, but failed to advance. The British troops were commanded by Major General Sir Edward M. Pakenham, brother-in-law of the duke of Wellington.

On January 1 General Pakenham ordered his artillery to blast out the Americans. Opposing the twenty-four British cannons were fourteen American guns, directed by Dominique You and manned by the Baratarian pirates. The pirates won. They silenced most of the British cannons, with the loss of three American guns. The British paused once more.

On the foggy morning of January 8, 1815, Pakenham gave the order for his troops, eight thousand strong, to advance. The American forces, fewer than six thousand, had taken positions north of the Rodriguez Canal, south of New Orleans. Their right flank was anchored on the Mississippi River, their left in a grove of cypress trees. A heavy frost covered the stubble of sugarcane, and Jackson, standing on a parapet, saw a field of red tunics crossed by white belts, seemingly endless, moving slowly and steadily toward him.

"Pick your targets and aim above the cross plates," the American officers called to their men.

Six hundred yards away. Five hundred yards. The Americans held their fire. Their rifles were not accurate beyond four hundred yards. The first American cannons blasted off and British cannons fired back. Smoke covered the battlefield. Jackson ordered his guns to cease fire, to give his riflemen a better field. When the smoke cleared, the solid red line of British troops was only three hundred yards away and running forward.

"Fire!"

The American riflemen shot in unison, then settled down to reload, while another group stepped up.

"Fire!"

Once more a volley of lead into the British ranks.

Then a third firing. The field was strewn with redcoats. "Never before had British veterans quailed," an English officer said later, "but it would be silly to deny that they did so now. That leaden torrent no man could face."

Pankenham himself was fatally wounded. The British retreated, but stout British soldiers re-formed their lines and advanced once more, with incredible bravery. They were mowed down again. The Americans were equally resolute, and they had a better position on the field. Twenty British soldiers reached the American defensive line, but that was all. The British were forced to retreat, and that for all practical purposes was the end of the battle.

Ironically enough, as is well known, the battle was fought after the Treaty of Ghent, which ended the war, was signed. But news of the peace did not reach either Washington or New Orleans until weeks later. Andy Jackson was acclaimed a hero, and he was generous enough to share his acclaim with the pirates of Barataria. They received pardons from President Madison.

The second war with England was over, on terms that gave neither side victory, but still things were not peaceful in Florida. Jackson had pacified the Indians there once; now they were again on the warpath. Spain still had legal ownership of both West and East Florida, and actual possession of East Florida. But the Americans knew that Spain, faced with revolution in all her western possessions, could not hold them. "As soon as our population gains a decided preponderance in those regions, Florida will hardly be considered by Spain as a part of her dominion," Monroe said.

In East Florida, adventurers of all nationalities were active on Amelia Island, near the St. Mary's River that formed the border between Georgia and Florida. Some of them tried to use the island as a base for raiding Spanish Florida and, perhaps, even South America. At one time, they even set up a semirepublic called the Northern Division of East Florida, but this collapsed because of internal differences and Spanish pressure. Soon after, the adventuresome leaders of Amelia Island annexed themselves to the Republic of Mexico and flew the Mexican flag, but this movement collapsed too, this time because of American pressure.

The Americans were roused to activity by the fact that the Seminole Indians just north of the Florida border refused to vacate lands given by Jackson, in the Treaty of Fort Jackson, to the Creek. The angry Seminole, pushed from their native lands, sought the aid of British agents in the area. The American army commander in Georgia was ordered to carry out an offensive against the Seminole, pursuing them into the Spanish territory of East Florida if necessary, but under no circumstances to take action against any Spanish fort.

On December 26, 1817, Jackson received orders to go to Georgia and "adopt the necessary measures to terminate the conflict" with the Indians. To Jackson, who had made no secret of his private feelings, this was an invitation to capture Florida. He wrote a letter to Monroe in which he said that "the whole of East Florida [can be] seized and this can be done without implicating the government." Afterward Jackson contended that he had received approval through a third party to do so.

On the morning of March 10, 1818, at Fort Scott in Georgia, near the Florida border, Jackson formally took command of an army of eight hundred regular troops and nine hundred Georgia militiamen. At noon the army set off through muddy trails, marching south. In five days they reached Negro Fort on the Apalachicola River, where Jackson received word that Indians had demanded arms from the Spanish commander of St. Marks to the east. He promptly marched there and lowered the Spanish flag, but the Indians had fled. He marched farther east, 107 miles, to the village of Chief Boleck on the Suwanee River, but the Indians had fled from there too. Jackson returned to St. Marks.

On these various marches, he had captured two Britons. One of them was Alexander Arbuthnot, a Scottish merchant, who had become friendly with the Indians of Suwanee and traded with them. The other was an English adventurer, Robert Christy Ambrister, who supported the Seminole. Jackson ordered them tried by a military court, Arbuthnot for inciting the Indians to war, giving aid to the enemy, and spying, and Ambrister for assuming command of Indians in a war with the United States.

Arbuthnot insisted that he had sold powder to the Indians, but for hunting only. Witnesses produced letters showing that he had appealed to the British for troops, arms, and ammunition to fight the Americans. He asked the judges to lean on the side of mercy. Ambrister pleaded guilty to the charge that he had assumed command of the Indians in a war with the United States, but he too asked for mercy. The military court rejected both pleas, and ordered Arbuthnot to be hanged and Ambrister to be shot. Jackson approved the sentence and it was carried out.

On May 7 Jackson's army marched from Negro Fort through mud and water west toward Pensacola. He captured that city on May 28, 1818, and the following day he appointed an army officer military and civil governor and declared that "the revenue laws of the United States" were now in effect. The military conquest of East and West Florida was complete. How would the diplomats seal this military victory, achieved in a time of technical peace?

5

The Pacific Beckons

THE AMERICAN MINISTER TO LONDON, John Quincy Adams, was listening to the British foreign minister, Lord Castlereagh.

"If the Floridas were ceded to the United States, what objection would they have to the Mississippi as a boundary?" Castlereagh asked. Britain was Spain's ally, but Castlereagh knew that the Spanish hold over the Floridas was ebbing rapidly as the wars of independence in South America shifted in favor of the insurgents. Still, it was his duty to his ally to intercede for her.

Adams had already repeated the American position that West Florida was part of the Louisiana Purchase, but now he pointed to the map on the wall. A wide range of territory east of the Mississippi was marked "Louisiana."

"That would be the objection," he said, and went on to assert that if Spain would be rational, the United States could easily come to an accommodation with her.

Castlereagh replied that he could say the same of the United States.

On the map in front of them, the United States clearly

showed the trend of the future. From the original thirteen colonies precariously perched on the Atlantic seaboard, the nation had now expanded to the Rocky Mountains. No matter that the actual boundary line in the west was not clearly defined; the nation was moving westward. People were picking up from New England and taking their families to Ohio; from Ohio, the more venturesome were moving toward Iowa and Missouri. It was only a matter of time until the lands to the west—vacant except for Indians, of course—would beckon to the adventuresome and land hungry, and the tide of migration would flow west until the Pacific was reached.

The United States already had a claim to the northwest, based on Captain Robert Gray's voyage in 1792, the Lewis and Clark expedition in 1805, and the settling of Astoria in 1811. In 1817 only the southwest and southeast corners of the United States—both owned by Spain—and the disputed northwest remained to be won before the nation would literally stretch from sea to sea.

Shortly after his conversation with Castlereagh, John Quincy Adams, the son of former President John Adams, who himself had been a diplomat, returned to the United States to become secretary of state. The United States was at peace with England and the rest of the world.

The only foreign problem in 1817 was with Spain. It involved the vexing question of Florida, which was tied up with colonial revolt in South America, Spanish fear of American recognition of the revolutionists, and a Spanish desire to establish and maintain a firm boundary between Mexico, her last major possession in North America, and the United States. To a clearheaded foreigner like Castlereagh, it was apparent that Spain had, for all practical purposes, lost Florida. What remained, then, was to drive the best possible bargain for Spain with the United States for the northern boundaries of

Mexico, which then included what is now Texas and the entire southwestern part of the United States.

As military action in Florida continued, Adams mentioned to the Spanish ambassador, Luis de Onís: "If we don't come to an early conclusion of the Florida negotiations, Spain won't have the possession of Florida to give us." In Madrid the Spanish had reluctantly come to the same conclusion: Florida would have to go. In return, Spain hoped for a Mexican boundary line as close to the Mississippi as possible and agreement by the United States not to recognize the rebellious South Americans.

Thus, late in 1817, the Spanish minister opened a series of negotiations with Adams, giving a long dissertation on the historic boundaries of Louisiana and Florida. The United States had no rights either east or west of the delta of the Mississippi, he said. The Americans earlier had claimed that the western border of Louisiana ran clear to the Rio Grande. Now Adams offered a concession: the line of the Colorado River from the Gulf of Mexico to its source and thence to Canada.

If this line had been accepted by Spain, it would have put the western border of the United States on the eastern slopes of the Rocky Mountains, cutting the country off from the northwest and the Pacific Ocean. But de Onís's instructions were such that he could not accept the American extension to the Colorado River. He did suggest another line, however, a little farther west of the Mississippi.

During these preliminary bargaining sessions, it was assumed that Florida would be ceded to the Americans. But now General Jackson had overturned the diplomatic card table; his small army had invaded Florida. De Onís demanded punishment of Jackson, an indemnity for the outrage, and Florida restored to Spanish sovereignty.

Despite this seemingly strong demand, the Spanish desire for peace was obvious and their position therefore weak. In conversations with Adams, de Onís learned that if Spain would yield Florida and all financial matters were settled, the United States would be content to let the western boundary question wait. This was precisely what de Onís did not want; his instructions were quite clear that he was not to make any settlement that did not include a western boundary.

"I will not advise His Majesty to make any settlement unless it fixes safe and permanent limits west of the Mississippi," he told Adams.

"If that's the way it is, we can take the Rio Grande for a frontier," Adams replied with a smile.

"Better still the Mississippi," de Onís said, also jokingly.

The two men used as the basis for their discussions the January 1, 1818, edition of Melish's Map of the United States and the Contiguous British and Spanish Possessions. On July 16, 1818, the bargaining got down to realistic details. Adams proposed a boundary starting at the Trinity River, from its mouth on the Gulf of Mexico to its source, then north to the Red River, following that to its source, then crossing to the Rio Grande to its source, and thence due west all the way to the Pacific. De Onís proposed a line farther east that would have cut off half of the Louisiana Purchase. He also demanded free navigation of the Mississippi and the Missouri.

"If he won't agree to reasonable terms, break off the negotiations," President Monroe, exasperated, instructed Adams.

Adams then made what he called a final offer to the Spanish: the Sabine River from the Gulf of Mexico to the Red River, then along the Red River to its source, then along the mountains to forty-one degrees north latitude, and then in a straight line to the Pacific.

De Onís had already achieved what Spain wanted; he had safeguarded the borders of Texas for Mexico. But he was a hard bargainer. He accepted the Sabine River line but suggested that a line be drawn due north to the Missouri River, a proposal that was completely unacceptable to the Americans.

Adams now seized on the opportunity of replying to a note from Spain protesting Jackson's invasion of Florida. On November 28, 1818, Adams sent a sharp reply, which one historian has called "the greatest state paper of John Quincy Adams' diplomatic career." He maintained that if Spain could not exercise responsible authority in Florida, she would have to cede the area to the United States. And then he said:

> The President will neither inflict punishment nor pass censure on General Jackson for that conduct, the motives of which were founded in the purest patriotism; of the necessity for which he had the most immediate and effectual means of forming a judgment; and the vindication of which is written on every page of the law of nations, as well as in the first law of nature—self defense. . . .
>
> Spain must immediately make her election, either to place a force in Florida adequate at once to the protection of her territory and to the fulfillment of her engagement, or cede to the United States a province of which she retains nothing but the nominal possession, but which is, in fact, a derelict, open to the occupancy of every enemy, civilized or savage, of the United States, and serving no other earthly purpose than as a post of annoyance to them.

The state paper disarmed critics of Monroe and Adams at home; silenced the British, who, to the astonishment of their own press and Europe, did not protest; and convinced the Spanish that there was no point in delaying their surrender. At the beginning of 1819, de Onís received instructions to sign a treaty. After five more weeks of bargaining, agreement was reached. The treaty provided the following:

Article 1: Peace and friendship between Spain and the United States

Article 2: The king of Spain ceded to the United States "all the territories which belong to him, situated to the eastward of the Mississippi, known by the name of East and West Florida"

Article 3: Fixed the boundary line between the two countries west of the Mississippi as follows: from the mouth of the Sabine River on the Gulf of Mexico, north along the western bank of the river to the thirty-second degree of latitude; then due north to the Red River; then west along the Red River to one hundred degrees west longitude; then due north to the Arkansas River; then to its source, at forty-two degrees of north latitude; then due west to the Pacific Ocean

The treaty was signed on February 22, 1819. That night Adams recorded in his diary:

The acquisition of the Floridas has long been an object of earnest desire to this country. The acknowledgement of a definite line of boundary to the South Sea forms a great epoch in our history. The first proposal of it in this negotiation was my own, and I trust it is now secured beyond the reach of revocation. It was not even among our claims by the Treaty of Independence with Great Britain. It was not even among our pretensions under the purchase of Louisiana—for that gave us only the range of the Mississippi and its waters. . . . It is the only peculiar and appropriate right acquired by this treaty in the event of its ratification. I record the first assertion of this claim for the United States as my own, because it is known to be mine perhaps only to the members of the present administration, and may perhaps never be known to the public—and if ever known, will soon and easily be forgotten.

On February 24 the Senate unanimously ratified the treaty and it was immediately signed by President Monroe. It took more than two years for the Floridas to become part of the United States in actual fact, however, largely because of the long delay by Spain in confirming the treaty. Finally, on July 10, 1821, General Jackson, acting for the United States, took formal possession of East Florida and a week later of West Florida.

The United States had completed its geographic form east of the Mississippi, and, more important, it had stretched out to the west and reached the Pacific—largely because of the efforts of John Quincy Adams. As Samuel Flagg Bemis, the historian, has said: "It was the greatest diplomatic victory won by a single individual in the history of the United States."

6

The Canadian Border

THE SIMPLE WORDS IN THE TREATY OF PEACE OF 1783 that defined the United States border with Canada caused disputes almost as soon as they were written. The lines that were so easily drawn on the best map of the period, Mitchell's map of 1755, were often difficult to follow through the forests, swamps, hills, and rivers of the territory itself, and at times seemed most illogical to local residents.

Attempts to determine the precise boundary lines brought about arguments, shootings, court suits, even actual invasion and war. Diplomats held conferences, commissioners were appointed, and a king mediated, to try to settle the disputes. Most of the major questions were settled by 1842, in the east at least. But even today there is an International Boundary Commission, whose job it is to maintain the United States–Canada border.

Let's take a look at how the boundary line developed, using as a beginning the words of the Treaty of 1783.

A line to be drawn along the middle of the river St. Croix from its mouth in the Bay of Fundy to its source. . . .

That seemed relatively simple, but before 1783 came to an end, it was discovered that the term "St. Croix River," which appeared on Mitchell's map, was not used locally. In fact, there were two different rivers, both known to the settlers by their Indian names, that might have been meant, the Magaguadavic to the east and the Schoodic to the west. The Americans claimed that the Magaguadavic was the boundary; the British said it was the Schoodic.

A large area of land between the rivers was at stake, but even more important, a further definition of the boundary depended on the source of the river. Messages between the governments of Britain and the United States failed to resolve the controversy. Finally, in 1794, the Jay Treaty provided for a commission of three to determine "what river was truly intended under the name of the river St. Croix."

The three men appointed met at St. Andrews in New Brunswick, Canada, on October 4, 1796, and began a survey of the area. Luckily, an excavation on an island in the Schoodic River revealed remnants of a camp erected there in 1604 by Samuel de Champlain's expedition. The commission thereupon voted to make the Schoodic River the boundary line, and called the river the St. Croix.

A vexing problem remained, however, because the river emptied into Passamaquoddy Bay, not the Bay of Fundy, as described in the treaty. Who owned the islands in Passamaquoddy Bay, then?

Direct negotiations failed to solve the problem, and, finally, in the Treaty of Ghent in 1814, the two countries appointed two commissioners to decide. On November 24, 1817, they reached a compromise, that "Moose Island, Dudley Island, and Frederick Island, in the Bay of Passamaquoddy, which is part of the Bay of Fundy, do each of them belong to the United States of America; and that all the other islands in the Bay of Passamaquoddy, and the island of Grand Manan in the Bay of Fundy do each of them belong to His Britannic Majesty."

. . . from the north west angle of Nova Scotia, viz, that angle which is formed by a line drawn due north from the source of the St. Croix River to the Highlands; along said highlands which divide those rivers that empty themselves into the river St. Lawrence, from those which fall into the Atlantic Ocean, to the northwesternmost head of Connecticut River. . . .

These words led to the most serious boundary dispute and almost caused a war. Commissioners had duly found the source of the St. Croix River and had marked a yellow birch tree hooped with iron to define the point. After that, however, disagreement led to argument, dispute to arrests and court orders; British and American troops came in; the state of Maine defied the British government; the king of the Netherlands made a decision that was rejected. Finally a bribe to an American diplomat led to peace on the border.

Even before 1800 the United States and Britain both recognized that different interpretations of the words of the treaty were possible, and several attempts were made to come to an agreement, but they failed. In the Treaty of Ghent at the end of the War of 1812, the two nations agreed to appoint commissioners to settle the dispute, with the proviso that if they did not agree, the question would be turned over to a friendly sovereign for arbitration.

The commissioners met in St. Andrews, New Brunswick, in 1816, and again in Boston in 1817. Their first step was to authorize surveyors to run a line due north from the source of the St. Croix to the "highlands." The surveyors agreed on

what direction north was, but little else. The American surveyor maintained that the north line ran 143 miles to the
watershed between the St. Lawrence and the Restigouche
River. The Briton maintained that the north line ended at
Mars Hill, about forty miles north of the St. Croix. His argument was that the treaty did not specify the precise point
at which the waters divided in the highlands, but merely the
highlands. Certainly Mars Hill was in the highlands, he said.
About twelve thousand square miles were in dispute. After
several years of fruitless argument, the two commissioners
met for the last time in New York in 1822, and agreed to
disagree.

The stage was set for international arbitration, but both
sides delayed. In 1826 Albert Gallatin, the United States minister to London, tried to reach agreement, but failed. A year
later both sides agreed to arbitrate; then it took three years
for them to agree on an arbitrator. William, king of the
Netherlands, was finally chosen.

In the disputed area, meanwhile, conditions were getting
worse, mainly because an American flag was raised on the
Fourth of July by an American citizen. The American, John
Baker, who had settled in the Madawaska area near the St.
John River in the northern part of the region, was seized by
a sheriff's posse from New Brunswick and charged with dis-
turbing the peace of the British province. Baker replied in
court that he was an American citizen living in the United
States and, therefore, not subject to a British court. The jury
found him guilty and the judge fined him £25, thus establishing the British assertion of jurisdiction.

On the diplomatic front, the situation was equally confused.
To add to the complexity, Maine, which had been part of
Massachusetts and was now a sovereign state, claimed the
disputed area for itself. Thus there were at least four parties

to the dispute: the state of Maine, the province of New Brunswick, the United States, and Great Britain—as well as the people who lived on the land. Almost everyone favored arbitration, except Maine, which believed that arbitration was "the delegation of sovereignty to a despot."

After listening to lengthy arguments, King William handed down his decision on January 10, 1831, in a lengthy document written in French. He found neither the British nor the American claim valid and set a compromise line somewhere in between. His suggested boundary line extended due north of the source of the St. Croix to the St. John River, up that river to the St. Francis River, and thence to the St. Lawrence watershed.

The British promptly accepted the proposal, although it gave the Americans about two thirds of the disputed area, because it allowed them enough land to build a military road into New Brunswick. But the Americans rejected it, on the grounds that the king had exceeded the terms of reference of the arbitration procedure.

The state of Maine thereupon took steps to assume possession. The legislature passed an act incorporating the Madawaska area as part of the state. New Brunswick authorities acted quickly. Three Americans were arrested and fined £50 each and sentenced to three months in jail by the New Brunswick Supreme Court for taking part in a Maine election. Maine reacted in 1837 by sending a census taker who seemed eager to be arrested and thus create another inflammatory incident. The New Brunswick authorities obliged. Maine ordered the state militia to be ready to go into action. The Aroostook War, undeclared and bloodless, had begun.

In January 1839 the governor of Maine authorized the arrest of all persons, especially illicit lumber cutters, in the disputed lands and sent a posse headed by Rufus McIntire to oust the

Canadians. But the Canadians surprised and captured some of the posse, including McIntire. Maine responded by voting $800,000 for military purposes and authorizing the draft of ten thousand men.

While the war of words and movement was being pushed in the north woods, in Washington the British minister and the United States secretary of state exchanged messages, each hoping the other would yield and end the dispute. Congress, on the other hand, reflecting its traditional fear of the British, passed a bill authorizing the president to raise volunteers for service in the north. President Van Buren, however, named General Winfield Scott as a special emissary to try to stop the impending war. At the same time, Maine's posse, numbering about ten thousand by now, built wooden fortifications and patrolled roads. The New Brunswick government also drafted local militia and sent out patrols.

General Scott, who had fought in the War of 1812 and who had pacified Indians by arms farther west, arrived in Maine in March 1839. He quickly discovered that the chief obstacle to peace was the rivalry between the two political parties in Maine, each of which was afraid to be accused of appeasement. However, by patient negotiating Scott won their confidence and also an agreement that they would not attempt to settle the dispute by force, if the Canadians would do the same.

It turned out that Scott and the local British commander were acquaintances, having fought against each other on the Niagara frontier. And the Briton was delighted to accept the compromise, which meant that Maine retained the Aroostook Valley and New Brunswick retained the upper St. John Valley for the time being. By the end of March both sides began to withdraw their troops and, still without a shot, the Aroostook War ended.

Once again it was time for the diplomats to act. The political climate in both countries had changed. In England the Liberal government had fallen and the more conciliatory Conservative party had taken office. As their negotiator, the British named Lord Ashburton, of the famous Baring banking family, a known friend of the United States. In Washington, Daniel Webster, who had ambitions to become the United States minister to the Court of St. James's, was secretary of state. What better way to assure his appointment than by clearing up the problems with Britain?

The negotiations began in Washington in June 1842, and there followed some rather odd maneuvers by the American secretary of state involving false maps, a Harvard historian, and even bribery.

The controversy could have been settled easily if an official copy of the Mitchell map used by the peace negotiators in 1783 had been available, for on it the boundary was marked in red. But apparently no copy was on hand. One of Webster's friends, Professor Jared Sparks of Harvard, had seen a copy of such a map in the archives of the French government. From memory he marked the line on a map of Maine and sent it to Webster. The problem for the Americans was that Sparks's map confirmed the British claims.

Surprisingly, this pleased Webster. The documents were just what he needed to convince the obstinate men of Maine and the northeast to compromise. Somehow the British contributed $14,000 for "traveling expenses," to compensate Sparks for a trip to Augusta, the capital of Maine, and other northern points, to lay his "evidence" before the local residents. As was pointed out by several people, $150 or so would have been enough to cover these expenses. Where the rest of the money went, nobody knows. In any case, Sparks made the trip, the Maine men were convinced, and the door was opened for the settlement of the dispute.

On August 9, 1842, the Webster-Ashburton Treaty was signed in Washington. The United States got less than it would have if it had accepted the arbitration award of the king of the Netherlands some eleven years before. The treaty defined the highlands in great detail, but the line gave five thousand square miles of the disputed area to Great Britain and seven thousand to the United States. It assured the British of their military highway from Montreal to New Brunswick (now Canada Route 2); it gave the United States some land in northern New Hampshire and New York (which will be discussed below); it more clearly defined the boundaries in the Great Lakes area (which will also be discussed below); and it stipulated that both governments would cooperate in suppressing the slave trade from Africa.

Three ironic events followed. First, Daniel Webster did not become minister to London, despite his machinations. Second, John Baker, the man who had raised the American flag on the Fourth of July in 1827, found that the new boundary line put his farm on the Canadian side, and he lived on in Canada and died there. Third, after the treaty was ratified, the British government discovered that it had in its archives King George III's copy of the Mitchell map used in the peace negotiations of 1783. On it was a distinct red line marked "boundary as described by Mr. Oswald" (the British negotiator of 1783). The line corresponded exactly to the American claims, which had been yielded by Daniel Webster.

. . . The northwesternmost head of the Connecticut river . . .

This seemed to be a perfectly clear-cut line, since one of the rivers in the area was called the Connecticut River—but here too was a cause of contention. A map of the New Hampshire–Canada border shows that the Connecticut River divides into four streams there: Hall's Stream, the farthest west; Indian Stream; Perry Stream; and the main branch of the Connecticut. The British claimed that the branch called the Connecticut was meant; the Americans claimed that the "northwesternmost head" meant the river that was farthest west, Hall's Stream. Under the Treaty of Ghent, commissioners were appointed, but they could not agree. The king of the Netherlands, the impartial arbitrator chosen by both sides, ruled in 1831 as part of his compromise that the boundary should be Indian Stream. His proposal was rejected in its entirety, however.

The area in dispute was rather small; it had no military value; its farmland was poor. To the settlers who lived there (fewer than one hundred families), however, it seemed that their rights were being treated too lightly by Britain and the United States, as well as by New Hampshire and the Province of Quebec. In June 1832 the local residents drafted a constitution and on July 9 proclaimed a new state. The vote was fifty-six to three. There were numerous scuffles between adherents of Canada and adherents of the United States, and finally, in November 1835, fifty militiamen from New Hampshire occupied the region. The settlers who supported Canadian rule were harassed until they left.

In the Webster-Ashburton negotiations of 1842, the Indian Stream area was a pawn. It was yielded by the British in return for other lands they received in the northeast. The "northernmost head" of the Connecticut River was defined as Hall's Stream, just what the Americans had asked for in the first place.

. . . the forty-fifth degree of north latitude . . . until it strikes the river Iroquois or Cataraquy [the St. Lawrence] . . .

What could be simpler than that? The line between New York State and Quebec had been surveyed and marked in 1771–1774 by Thomas Valentine, principal surveyor for Quebec, and John Collins, principal surveyor for New York. The peace negotiators on both sides agreed to accept the line. Why then a controversy? The line, it turned out, was not accurate. It was discovered a few years later that the line marked by Valentine and Collins was not the forty-fifth parallel.

Under the provisions of the Treaty of Ghent, two commissioners, one from each side, were appointed to survey the line again and come to an agreement. They reported that at the northern end of Lake Champlain, near Rouses Point, New York, the border was three-quarters of a mile north of a true forty-five-degree line and that the United States fort there was actually a quarter of a mile north of forty-five degrees and therefore in British territory. After that, the United States claimed the Valentine-Collins line as the border; the British insisted that the forty-five-degree line was the border. On this too, the king of the Netherlands was called to arbitrate. He ruled in favor of the British, with one exception. He said that the border should be drawn to include the fort at Rouses Point within the United States.

After his recommendations were rejected, the issue lay dormant until the Webster-Ashburton negotiations, when the region, like the Indian Stream region, was a bargaining point for the British. They yielded on the issue, which was unimportant to them, and accepted the Valentine-Collins line. Today, for 154 miles, the northern border of New York and Vermont arches slightly above the forty-fifth degree of north latitude, and Rouses Point, north of forty-five degrees, is on United States soil.

*. . . along the middle of said [St. Lawrence] river into Lake
Ontario . . .*

The waters of the five Great Lakes pour through the eastern
end of Lake Ontario into the St. Lawrence River and thence
to the ocean. The area where the lake water joins the river
is known as the Thousand Islands, which actually encompass
about fifteen hundred islands in the St. Lawrence between
Canada and New York State.

If there were no islands, it would be easy to find the middle
of the river. But like all the seemingly simple definitions on
the map, this one too posed difficulties for the surveyors on
the ground. Under the provisions of the Treaty of Ghent in
1814, the British and the Americans sought a solution to the
problem. In Article VI of the treaty they took note of the fact
that doubts had arisen as to what was the middle of the St.
Lawrence River (and of the Great Lakes as well) and referred
the dispute to two commissioners, one for each side, for a
final determination.

The commissioners, with astronomers and surveyors, met
at St. Regis, New York, in the spring of 1817. At the start,
they agreed on one ticklish problem, that the boundary line
should run through water wherever possible. If an island was
found in the middle of the proposed line, the boundary would
go on one side or the other, on the water, so that no island
would be shared by the two countries. Island by island, they
considered the problem, making individual decisions in each
case.

The commissioners made their report in 1822, having
reached a compromise on most of their differences. They
awarded Grand Island near Kingston to the British, for example, and Long Sault Islands near Cornwall to the United
States. Today the Thousand Islands are some on one side of
the border, some on the other.

. . . through the middle of said lake [Ontario] until it strikes
the communication of water between that lake and Lake Erie;
through the middle of said lake, until it strikes at the water
communication between that lake and Lake Huron; thence
along the middle of said water communication into the Lake
Huron; thence through the middle of said lake to the water
communication between that lake and Lake Superior, thence
through Lake Superior northward of the Isles Royal . . .

The commissioners finished their survey of the St.
Lawrence in 1818 and then proceeded into the Great Lakes.
They usually worked in the summer, retiring to New York or
Montreal in the winter to draw and check their maps. They
had few problems with drawing lines across the middle of the
large lakes; the only disputes concerned the water arteries
between the lakes. One of these involved the Detroit River
between Lakes Erie and Huron, and three specks of land,
Fox, Sugar, and Stony Islands, as well as one island, Bois
Blanc. Both sides claimed them all. The decision was that the
United States could have the three specks and Britain could
have Bois Blanc Island, which was closer to the Canadian
shore. This finding was part of the report the commissioners
filed in 1822.

. . . to the Long Lake; thence through the middle of said
Long Lake, and the water communications between it and the
Lake of the Woods to the said Lake of the Woods; thence
through the said lake to the most northwestern point
thereof . . .

Once again, the maps played false with the surveyors. When
the two commissioners left the western shores of Lake
Superior, they were moving into areas where only the voyageurs and Indians had trod. There was no such body of water

as the Long Lake, the key connection between Lake Superior and Lake of the Woods as shown on their maps. At first glance it seemed clear to both parties (as to anyone who looks at an accurate map today) that what was meant was the Pigeon River route up to Rainy Lake and then to Lake of the Woods. But logic was thrown overboard as each side attempted to gain the most from the obvious mistake.

Egged on by the Canadian fur-trading interests, who vitally needed free transit at Grand Portage on the Pigeon River, the British commissioner suggested that what the treaty makers meant was the largest river draining into Lake Superior from the west. That obviously was the St. Louis River, which reached Lake Superior at its southwest corner. The American commissioner, who was positive that the Pigeon River was clearly what was intended, felt that he could meet the British challenge only by moving the suggested boundary far to the north, as a bargaining ploy. He proposed that the boundary should start at the Kaministikwia River, just north of Isles Royal.

The two commissioners surveyed the land in 1825 and submitted a report of disagreement in 1827. Thus, like so many of the other boundary disputes, this remained for Webster and Ashburton to settle in 1842. They did so by agreeing to the Pigeon River line, which was clearly the line intended from the start. British obstinacy had one favorable result for them, however. There was a stipulation in the agreement that all water communications in the area would be open and free to both countries. They also agreed that the northwesternmost point of Lake of the Woods was at latitude 49°23' N and longitude 95°14' W. Today that is the most northern point of the conterminous United States (the forty-eight states), a little peninsula of the United States that juts out of Canada. It is

150 square miles, separated from the rest of the state of Minnesota by Lake of the Woods and called the Northwest Angle State Park.

> *. . . from thence on a due west course to the river Mississippi . . .*

This was one of the grossest mistakes of the treaty of 1783: the Mississippi was not west of Lake of the Woods but south. The error was once again based on Mitchell's map, which did not show the source of the Mississippi but merely said that it was supposed to "arise about the fiftieth degree latitude," or a little to the north of Lake of the Woods.

When John Jay concluded his treaty with the British in 1794, Article 4 pointed out that "it is uncertain whether the River Mississippi extends so far to the Northward as to be intersected by a Line to be drawn due West from Lake of the Woods in a manner mentioned in the Treaty of Peace between His Majesty and the United States." The Jay Treaty went on to provide for a survey of the river and, if the river was not intersected by such a line, for negotiations to settle the dispute amicably. The joint survey was never made. But in 1798 David Thompson, the foremost surveyor for the fur-trading Canadian North West Company, discovered that the source of the Mississippi was 47°39′ N latitude, well below the lake. Thus it was evident that there was a gap in the northern boundary.

In 1803 the British foreign secretary, Lord Hawkesbury, and the American minister, Rufus King, agreed on a treaty that among other things would have granted to the British a line south from Lake of the Woods to the Mississippi. This would have put the United States–Canada border 152 miles south of the forty-ninth parallel (and certainly might have set a precedent for the northernmost limits of the United States west of the Mississippi). Under the leadership of John Quincy Adams, the United States Senate rejected that part of the agreement.

Unknown to the negotiators in London, a far greater territorial agreement was in the making in Paris at about the same time, the Louisiana Purchase. When that agreement was concluded, however, many mysteries about Louisiana remained unsolved—among them, its boundaries. Louisiana was supposed to comprise the region drained by the Mississippi River, but as one Frenchman commented, "the line of demarcation has not been determined toward the northeast, as well as toward the north, where it is lost in the vast wilderness in which there is no European settlement and in which it seems that even the necessity for boundaries is unknown."

President Jefferson had contended, erroneously it turned out, that the Treaty of Utrecht between France and England in 1713 had agreed on the forty-ninth parallel as the boundary. One of the virtues of this position was that it included within the territory claimed by the United States the watershed of the Red River of the North, which drained into Hudson's Bay. If the United States had insisted on substituting "the area of the Mississippi watershed," it would have conceded the Red River area (a large part of what is now Minnesota). The British seemed to have accepted the boundary supposedly set by the Treaty of Utrecht, but negotiations dragged on for years.

Early in 1818 Britain and the United States agreed to neutralize the waters of the Great Lakes and to provide for an unfortified frontier between the United States and Canada. Charles Bagot, the British minister to the United States, met with Richard Rush, acting secretary of state for the United States, and on April 28, 1818, signed the Rush-Bagot

Agreement. This sharply restricted the naval vessels of each country authorized along the United States–Canada border to half a dozen small boats, suitable only for customs patrolling, and ordered the dismantling of all other armed ships.

Later in 1818 Albert Gallatin, the United States minister to France, and Richard Rush, the American minister to Britain, met with an English negotiating team to consider many problems, among them the vexing northwest boundary dispute. They agreed on October 20, 1818, to ignore the question of the source of the Mississippi and to draw the boundary line due west on the forty-ninth parallel. This is how they worded their agreement:

> It is agreed that a line drawn from the most northwestern point of the Lake of the Woods, along the forty-ninth parallel of north latitude, or, if said point shall not be in the forty-ninth parallel of north latitude, then a line shall be drawn from the said point due north or south as the case may be, until the said line shall intersect the said parallel of north latitude, and from the point of such intersection due west along and with the said parallel shall be the line of demarcation between the territories of the United States, and those of His Britannic Majesty, and that said line shall form the northern boundary of the said territories of the United States, and the southern boundary of the territories of His Britannic Majesty, from the Lake of the Woods to the Stony Mountains.

That ended the long series of disputes between the United States and Britain about the border between the United States and Canada—as far west as "the Stony Mountains." From the Rockies to the Pacific would be another, and much more bitter, chapter. But the new struggle opened with a compromise. In 1818 negotiators from the two nations agreed:

. . . that any country that may be claimed by either party on the northwest coast of America, westward of the Stony Mountains, shall, together with its harbors, bays and creeks, and the navigation of all rivers within the same, be free and open, for the term of ten years from the date of the signature of the present convention, to the vessels, citizens, and subjects of the two Powers.

7

Texas

ON THE TWENTY-EIGHTH DAY OF FEBRUARY, 1836, a dust-covered courier galloped into the frontier settlement on the Brazos River where the Texas constitutional convention was about to meet. He had an ominous message:

> *Commandancy of the Alamo*
> *F'by 24th 1836*
>
> To the People of Texas: . . .
> I am besieged by a thousand or more of the Mexicans under Santa Anna. I have sustained a continual Bombardment & Cannonade for 24 hours. . . . The enemy has demanded a surrender. . . . I shall never surrender or retreat. I call on you in the name of Liberty, or patriotism & everything dear to the American character, to come to our aid with all dispatch. . . . If this call is neglected, I am determined to sustain myself as long as possible. . . . I die like a soldier who never forgets what is due to his own honor & that of his country—VICTORY OR DEATH.
>
> *W. Barret Travis*
> *Lt. Col. comdt.*

The war for Texan independence was several months old. In 1835, after several years of turmoil, the province of Texas had revolted against the Republic of Mexico. The vast area of Texas, from the Sabine River west to New Mexico, had belonged to Mexico since the days of the Spanish conquistadores. The people who lived there, in scattered towns and homesteads, were largely American, mainly refugees of one sort or another from the United States, soldiers of fortune, adventurers, gamblers, pirates, men and women ruined by scandal at home, and a few farmers. Most of them lived in the fertile coastal plain between the Sabine River and the Nueces River, the traditional southern boundary of Texas. Almost all of them wanted self-government, under Mexican rule if possible and, if not, then either independently or as part of the United States. Mexico reacted to this growing movement for independence by sending troops in 1830 to safeguard its territory. After a series of military maneuvers that lasted for years, the Texans in 1835 forced the Mexican troops back.

Sam Houston, commander of the tiny Texas army, warned that the Mexicans would be back as soon as General Antonio López de Santa Anna, who had been elected president of Mexico in 1833 and was now a dictator, could raise another force. Houston recommended that the small Texas detachment at San Antonio de Bexar destroy its weak fortifications and retire to the east to join the main Texas force. But the Texans, then as now sure that they could lick any man or any army, thought such advice was defeatist. So it was that Lieutenant Colonel William Barret Travis, a twenty-seven-year-old lawyer, with about one hundred and fifty men under his command, stayed firmly put in San Antonio.

On February 23, 1836, Santa Anna and his army, numbering six thousand men, arrived in front of San Antonio. The Texans could have retreated safely, but, confident of their

An equestrian portrait of Sam Houston, painted by S. Seymour Thomas. *San Jacinto Museum of History Association.*

own prowess, they moved instead into the two-story Alamo Mission, protected by thick stone walls. Santa Anna demanded their surrender. A cannon shot answered him. Travis sent out couriers, asking for reinforcements, and prepared to fight. So did Santa Anna, who told one of his generals: "You know that in this war there are no prisoners."

When the message from Travis in the Alamo reached the little settlement of Washington on the Brazos River, a constitutional convention was meeting in a large, unheated shed owned by a gunsmith. Fifty-nine delegates, only ten of whom had lived in Texas for more than six years, were drafting a declaration of independence, which was adopted on March 2, 1836, by chance the forty-third birthday of Sam Houston, the most prominent citizen of Texas. The delegates also had to consider what to do about "the large mercenary army, now advancing to carry on against us a war of extermination." To meet this military challenge, they named Houston commander-in-chief of the armies of the new republic, with the rank of major general.

On March 6 another message arrived from the beleaguered Alamo. Travis wrote:

> The spirits of my men are still high, although they have had much to depress them. We have contended for ten days against an enemy whose number are variously estimated at from fifteen hundred to six thousand men. . . . I hope your honorable body will hasten on reinforcements. . . . Our supply of ammunition is limited.

A member of the convention immediately moved that it adjourn and march to the relief of the Alamo. Houston called the resolution "madness." The function of the convention was to create a government for the Republic of Texas, he said. He himself, as commander of the army, would go to the Alamo to attempt to save the men, who were in an untenable position there because they had defied his orders to leave. He sent a message to another volunteer Texas force, under James W. Fannin, at Goliad on the Perdido Creek. Then Houston mounted his horse and, accompanied by three aides, rode west.

Before daybreak on that same day, Sunday, March 6, Santa Anna and his troops opened their final drive to take the Alamo. The defenders were weary from lack of sleep, after thirteen days of siege. They repulsed two attacks, but the Mexicans, ignoring heavy losses, attacked again. The Texans drooped from exhaustion; their ammunition ran out; they fought with clubs and knives. But it was hopeless. The Mexicans rushed in and ran from room to room, shooting anyone who was still alive. In a few hours it was all over. Every Texan in the Alamo was dead: Travis, Jim Bowie, Davy Crockett, and the rest. The Mexicans spared only about thirty women, children, and slaves. The victors themselves had lost about fifteen hundred men.

Five days after the battle was over, Houston reached Gonzalez on the Guadalupe River, about seventy miles east of San Antonio, and took command of almost four hundred volunteers. He had heard nothing of the Alamo massacre. Before he could move, the plainsman and hunter Deaf Smith (after whom a county in Texas is named) rode in with three survivors: Mrs. Suzanna Dickenson, whose husband had died in the Alamo; her fifteen-month-old daughter, Angelina; and a servant named Joe.

When the fighting had ended, Mrs. Dickenson, her clothing red with the blood of dying men, had been taken before Santa Anna and had been asked to bring a message to Houston. Tell him, Santa Anna said, that the story of the Alamo would be the story of all who rebelled against the authority of Mexico.

The rebels would be spared only if they laid down their arms and halted the fighting immediately. These, of course, were fighting words to any Texan.

Convinced that he could not fight the Mexicans where they were strong, Houston began to retreat. He planned to fall back to East Texas, hoping that the pursuing enemy would split his forces, thus giving the small Texas army a chance to defeat the much larger Mexican force. On the Brazos, meanwhile, the constitutional convention had elected as its president David S. Burnet, who carried a pistol in one pocket and a Bible in the other pocket of his black frock coat. Then the convention too decided to retreat; it moved the capital of the new republic to Harrisburg on the Buffalo Bayou.

Houston's reputation and the great danger to Texas brought him new recruits as he moved his army east across the Colorado River, pursued by Mexican patrols. Houston and his men marched through the dust and the rain, grumbling as soldiers always do. As the retreat continued, grumbling and desertions mounted. By the end of March, Houston had only nine hundred men left.

The cause of Texas suffered another shock then; another Texas force had been massacred. Fannin, commanding more than three hundred men, had dallied in Goliad until he was surrounded by superior Mexican forces and then had surrendered. The Mexicans, following Santa Anna's orders, executed them all as rebels.

The only hope for the survival of the Republic of Texas was Sam Houston and his nine hundred men. Houston had been raised in Tennessee, where he had become friendly with the Cherokee Indians, gaining the nickname of the Raven, before serving as a junior officer in the United States Army under Jackson in the war against the Creek in 1814. After he resigned from the army, he became a lawyer in Nashville, a major general of the state militia, a member of the House of Representatives, then governor of the state of Tennessee. In 1829, after his marriage of a few months broke up, he fled to the West to build a new life.

His military opponent, Santa Anna, was about the same age, forty-two. He had been a soldier since he was seventeen, fighting in the war for Mexican independence from Spain and in the numerous civil wars that followed. He was tall for a Mexican, five feet, ten inches, a flamboyant dresser, an effective speaker, a political opportunist. He maneuvered himself into power, starting as a liberal and then entrenching himself by catering to reactionary interests. He called himself the "Napoléon of the West," and like his model, he abolished constitutional government as soon as he could and established himself as a dictator. He was determined to punish the Texas rebels and confident of his ability to do so.

Now he was on the march to wipe out Houston's army. On April 7, 1836, Santa Anna captured San Felipe de Austin. One week later he took the Texas capital, Harrisburg, but the government had fled. The only men he captured were three printers putting out the only newspaper in Texas, the *Telegraph and Texas Observer*. Santa Anna burned the town. On April 18 he captured New Washington on Galveston Bay; the next day he burned it. Then he turned north.

San Houston had been training his ragtag army. Buckskin breeches were the nearest thing to a uniform his soldiers had. Some of them wore boots, some moccasins, some were barefoot; some wore Mexican sombreros, some slouch hats, some even wore black stovepipe hats. Houston revamped his units, trying to instill some sort of military discipline. He drilled, inspected, organized small maneuvers. But despite his efforts, there was an air of defeatism about the camp. Men got word that their families were fleeing, and some left to help them. President Burnet sent a brief message:

> Sir:
> The enemy are laughing you to scorn. You must retreat no more. The country expects you to fight.

On April 18 Houston moved his army to the Buffalo Bayou, just north of Harrisburg, and there he made his first speech to his weary and dispirited troops. Sitting on his big white stallion, Saracen, Houston said:

"Victory is certain! Trust in God and fear not! The victims of the Alamo and the names of those who were murdered at Goliad cry out for cool, deliberate vengeance. Remember the Alamo! Remember Goliad!"

"Remember the Alamo!" his men shouted back. One of the most famous phrases in American history had been born.

The next day the troops crossed the Buffalo Bayou, riding across on crude rafts. At nightfall the Texas army camped in a forest of oak trees dripping with Spanish moss, near the junction of the Buffalo Bayou and the San Jacinto River. The army was itching for a fight.

The morning of April 20 was cloudy and chilly. The two armies confronted each other on the plains of San Jacinto, with Santa Anna braced for an attack and Houston waiting. All that happened that day was an exchange of artillery fire and the making of a new Texas hero with the improbable name of Mirabeau Buonaparte Lamar. He was a young Georgian, a private in the cavalry. Twice that day Lamar showed incredible bravery under fire, once rescuing Thomas Jefferson Rusk, the secretary of war, who was surrounded by Mexican dragoons, and then rescuing a wounded comrade from Mexican lances. The next morning Lamar was promoted to the rank of colonel and given command of a cavalry unit.

A bugle sounded reveille on the morning of April 21, 1836, a day that was to become famous in the history of Texas. As morning broke, Houston lay sleeping under a saddle blanket, his head resting on a coil of rope. Santa Anna was restless; he was up early, carefully examining the Texas camp through a spyglass. He was satisfied with his position, though some of his generals pointed out that the enemy could hide in the woods at his left.

At nine o'clock in the morning a column of five hundred Mexican troops arrived in camp, bringing the Mexican force to more than thirteen hundred men. Houston had about eight hundred at his command. His men were growing restless, they were there to fight, but Houston was in no hurry. At noon, for the first time in the campaign, he called a council of war. Houston asked whether the army should attack or await a Mexican attack. Many of his aides, who had been impatient to fight, now expressed caution. Houston made no comment.

Shortly after three o'clock Houston finally ordered his men into two long skirmish lines nine hundred yards long and two men deep and prepared to attack. At four o'clock Houston, mounted on Saracen and wearing a slouch hat, a mud-spattered black frock coat, and brown pantaloons tucked into black boots, trotted to the front of the line and in a deep voice called out: "Trail arms. Forward!"

For ten long minutes the Texans moved quietly through the tall grass toward Santa Anna's camp. Occasionally a soft voice was heard: "Hold your fire, men." In the Mexican camp there was complete silence. Not a Mexican sentry was in sight. It was an astonishing spectacle. The Mexican camp was completely unprotected.

The firing began when the Texans reached to within forty

yards of the Mexican light fortifications. Cannons roared, rifles crackled, and the Texans swept forward, yelling: "Remember the Alamo! Remember Goliad!" The Texans charged into the sleepy Mexican camp, shouting, shooting, and using their knives. A handful of Mexicans fired back. One of these volleys hit Saracen, who crumpled to the ground. Houston, uninjured, jumped off, mounted another horse. In a brief time that horse was shot out from under him too, and Houston himself was wounded. A bullet hit him on the right leg, just above the ankle, breaking both bones. But he mounted a third horse and continued to fight.

Suddenly the fighting was all over. The Mexicans fled in all directions, many of them screaming: *"Me no Alamo."* Six Texans had been killed in the assault and twenty-four had been wounded. Among the Mexicans, more than six hundred were killed, about two hundred wounded, and almost seven hundred captured. In eighteen minutes the Battle of San Jacinto ended, a resounding victory for Houston and Texas.

What had happened to the Mexicans? They obviously had been taken by surprise. One story had it that Santa Anna had been taking a siesta in his tent, entertaining a young slave girl named Emily. He himself later said that he was resting from a hard day. Whatever the actual story, one thing was clear: Santa Anna had lost the battle and had fled from the battlefield. The Texans rounded up prisoners all day and had to be restrained from killing them. But there was no sign of the Mexican commander.

The next afternoon Houston sat with his back against a tree as his wound was being dressed. A patrol rode up with another captured Mexican for the prisoner compound: *"¡El presidente! ¡El presidente!"* Santa Anna, looking like a bedraggled ordinary soldier, had been captured; he had been hiding in a nearby swamp.

In this painting by William Huddle, Santa Anna is brought before the wounded Sam Houston, who offers the defeated general a seat on an ammunition box. *Archives Division, Texas State Library.*

He was brought before Houston. He bowed.

"I am Antonio López de Santa Anna, president of Mexico, commander-in-chief of the army of operations, and I put myself at the disposition of the brave General Houston," he said in Spanish. "I wish to be treated as a general should when a prisoner of war."

"General Santa Anna, have a seat," Houston replied, waving to an ammunition box.

The two men began to talk through an interpreter.

"That man may consider himself born to no common destiny who has conquered the Napoléon of the West," Santa Anna said. "And now it remains for him to be generous to the vanquished."

"You should have remembered that at the Alamo," Houston said.

Santa Anna's life was in peril. Bloodthirsty Texans stood listening to the conversation, stony-eyed. The Mexican general trembled.

"I summoned them to surrender," he said. "They refused. The Alamo was taken by storm. The usages of war justified what I did. I was acting under the orders of my government."

"You are the government of Mexico," Houston said coldly. "A dictator, sir, has no superior."

The Mexican officers around Santa Anna then asked about a point that had been puzzling them. "You were lucky, General Houston," they said, "that you did not fight us on the twentieth. Our men were ready then and so anxious to fight, we could hardly keep them in the ranks. Why did you wait, General, until after General Cos had reinforced us to attack?"

"Why take two bites for one cherry?" said Houston.

In the conversation that followed, the two commanders and their aides discussed the terms of a peace. Houston demanded the immediate evacuation of Mexican troops from the area. Santa Anna agreed and sent orders for the rest of his army to withdraw.

Santa Anna escaped with his life. The Texans under Houston had won a greater prize—their independence. Now it was up to the diplomats to secure that independence. On May 4, President Burnet, a political opponent of Houston's, arrived to conduct the negotiations. The following day Houston resigned his commission, to seek medical treatment of his infected wounds. And there ensued a most incredible scene of petty behavior on the part of the president of Texas.

On May 7, as Burnet and his party prepared to take Santa

Anna back to Galveston by ship, Houston was carried on a cot to the dockside. Burnet then issued an amazing order. Since Houston was no longer a government employee, said Burnet, he could not travel on the government ship. Texas officials regarded their president with astonishment. And the captain of the ship said bluntly: "This ship is not sailing unless General Houston is on it." It sailed, and Houston went on to New Orleans for medical attention.

A week later, on May 14, the Texans signed two treaties with Santa Anna. One, made public, provided that the Mexican troops would retreat south to the Rio Grande. The second treaty, kept secret, provided that Santa Anna, once he returned to Mexico, would use his influence to have the independence of Texas recognized.

Despite these agreements, Burnet was powerless to prevent the kidnapping of Santa Anna by Texans who thought his punishment should be more severe. They wanted to avenge the Alamo by executing him. A letter from Houston stopped that. "Santa Anna living may be of incalculable advantage to Texas in her present crisis," he wrote.

His prestige and power gone, Burnet called for an election to choose a new president. The new nation voted on September 5, 1836. Houston received 5,119 votes; Henry Smith, 745; and Stephen F. Austin, the man who had brought most of the American settlers into Texas in the early years, 587.

On October 22, 1836, Houston took the oath of office as president, and drawing the sword he wore at San Jacinto, he said: "It now, sir, becomes my duty to make a presentation of this sword, the emblem of my past office. I have worn it with some humble pretension in the defense of my country; and should my country call, I expect to resume it."

One of his first acts was to release Santa Anna and send

him back to Mexico, grateful that his life had been spared and pledged to recognize the independence of Texas. Once he was back in Mexico, however, the Mexican government declared the pledge "null and void and of no effect."

From the beginning, the Texans believed that they would be recognized by the United States and eventually would become part of the union. In the election in which Houston became president, the Texans voted six thousand for annexation, with less than a thousand opposed. But in the United States, President Jackson, who personally favored annexation, told Congress that "recognition at this time would scarcely be consistent with that prudent reserve with which we have heretofore held ourselves bound to treat all similar questions." A Texas emissary to Washington pleaded for recognition, but it was not until March 3, 1837, the last day of Jackson's term, that he appointed a minor diplomat to go to Texas, an action that was warmer than a cold shoulder but less than full recognition. It was clear to Houston that Texas would have to stand alone, at least for the time being.

What was Texas in this, the first year of its independence? Geographically speaking, the Texas legislature on December 19, 1836, defined its borders as follows:

Beginning at the mouth of the Sabine River, and running west along the Gulf of Mexico three leagues from land, to the mouth of the Rio Grande, thence due north to the forty-second degree of north latitude, thence along the boundary line as defined in the treaty between the United States and Spain [see Chapter 5] to the beginning.

Looking at a map, you can see that this definition of Texas included parts of what are now the states of New Mexico, Colorado, Wyoming, Kansas, and Oklahoma. It also included the area between the Nueces River and the Rio Grande, a claim that was bitterly disputed by Mexico, which regarded the Nueces as the proper border of Texas (which it was when Spain had owned Texas). Most of the area to the north and west was Indian land, the home of the Cherokee, the Comanche, and the Apache. The settled part of Texas was along the coastal plain in the southeast corner, from the Sabine River in the east to the Nueces and Rio Grande in the south, running inland from the Gulf of Mexico only a little more than a hundred miles.

The population was about fifty thousand, thirty thousand of whom were originally from the United States. There were about five thousand blacks, as many Mexicans, and about twelve thousand Indians, most of them hostile. Though the geographic borders set by the new nation included New Mexico, with a population of about fifteen thousand, in reality the Mexicans held it firmly. The vast area of Texas was sparsely settled, with great distances between settlements and small villages. The government was deeply in debt, political feuds divided its leaders, and many foreign countries were dubious about the stability of the country. It was in this atmosphere that the new nation had to grow and prosper.

Sam Houston arrived in his new capital, which was named after him, in April 1837. The city of Houston consisted of several log cabins, three taverns, and a few tents. Carpenters were busy at work, felling trees and building a capitol to house the government.

Congress met on May 5 and heard a message from President Houston. "We now occupy the proud title of a sovereign and independent Republic," he said, "which will impose on us the obligation of evincing to the world that we are worthy to be free." Congress and the president set about their work: They established a currency and took steps to stabilize it; they began to build ships for a navy; they sent envoys to negotiate treaties of commerce with Britain and France; they set up a customs systems.

Despite these moves to create a nation, the Texans would have preferred annexation to the United States. That seemingly simple matter of expansion, which everybody favored, was caught up in the complex problem of the balance between the slave and nonslave states of the United States. Senator John Calhoun of South Carolina, expressing the view of the Southern interests, told the Senate that "there are powerful reasons why Texas should be part of this Union." His meaning was clear: another slave state. On the other hand, the legislature of Vermont expressed the Northern point of view; it protested the admission of any state "whose constitution tolerates domestic slavery."

At the time the United States was neatly balanced between slave and nonslave states. Arkansas and Michigan had just been admitted, which meant there were thirteen slave states and an equal number of nonslave states. Three territories were on the verge of becoming states: Florida, the only slave territory; and Wisconsin and Iowa, both nonslave areas.

The situation was summed up by a resolution passed by the Alabama legislature late in 1837: "It needs but a glance at the map to satisfy the most superficial observer that an overbalance is produced by the extreme northeast, which as regards territory would be happily corrected and counterbalanced by the annexation of Texas." A resolution to do so had been introduced in Congress the previous year, but President Martin Van Buren and many other politicians were anxious to muffle the potentially dangerous slave question for the time being. Besides, 1837 was a year of financial panic and there were other more pressing issues.

The internal situation in Texas was relatively quiet. The hostile Indians were at peace. Mexico made no threatening gestures, although it refused to recognize Texas. Houston stepped down from the presidency in December 1838 and was succeeded by Mirabeau Buonaparte Lamar. In Lamar's administration the population continued to grow, and so did the problems. The public debt mounted, currency fell in value. Lamar mounted an expedition to take possession of Santa Fe, but the local residents repulsed it. After three years of his term of office, Texas, once more facing disaster, called on Houston. He was elected president for the second time and took office in December 1841 in Austin, now the capital. "It seems we have arrived at a crisis," he said.

Immediately he reduced his own salary from $10,000 to $5,000 a year, and cut the government payroll. He sent a peace mission to the Indians of the north, who were threatening to go on the warpath. He made plans to expand the army because Santa Anna, who seemed to pop in and out of power in Mexico like a jumping jack, was again making threatening moves. Mexico would soon plant her eagle standard on the banks of the Sabine, Santa Anna said. To this, Houston replied: "Ere the banner of Mexico shall float on the banks of the Sabine, the Texan standard of the single star, borne by the Anglo-Saxon race, shall display its bright folds in liberty's triumph on the Isthmus of Darien."

After this exchange of verbal taunts, a Mexican force raided San Antonio in September 1842, capturing some of its residents. Houston sent off an army of twelve hundred to raid Mexico. It reached the Rio Grande and then, as in all Texas armies, quarrels broke out. Most of the men went home, but three hundred crossed the river on a private raiding expedition and were promptly captured. England and France interceded for the prisoners, a truce was declared, and the Texans were freed.

The fledgling republic had sent envoys to England and

France, as well as to the United States. If the United States would not annex Texas, then perhaps the best hope was a guarantee of Texan freedom by the powers of Europe, Houston reasoned. He was aware that if negotiations with the United States failed, England and France might become neutral, leaving Texas to face a strong and vengeful Mexico.

The two European nations toyed with the various possibilities. After all, an independent Texas would be a barrier between the expanding United States and the markets of Latin America and would be an independent source of the important cotton crop. One thing held them back: friendship for Mexico and the knowledge that no Mexican politician, in office or out, could acknowledge the independence of the lost province and survive.

However, in the United States the atmosphere was changing, chiefly for two reasons: fear of British influence on Texas and fear among Southerners that Texas might go along with the growing abolitionist movement and become nonslave. Late in 1843 President John Tyler indicated that the United States would be happy to reopen the annexation question. Houston doubted, however, whether the necessary two-thirds vote could be obtained in the Senate. He played coy but instructed his envoys in Washington to negotiate a treaty if they could.

By April the treaty was ready and on April 12, 1844, it was signed and sent to a rambunctious Senate. Southern Senators favored quick annexation, before Texas could change its mind on what to them was the overriding question of the day, slavery. The North was split. Many Americans felt that it was the destiny of the United States to expand from sea to sea and that Texas was naturally a part of the country. Several of the Northern state legislatures argued, however, that annexation of a foreign country was unconstitutional. The treaty failed to get the necessary two-thirds vote, just as Houston had predicted.

Annexation became a major issue in the presidential campaign of 1844. James K. Polk, the candidate of the Democratic party, had as one of his planks the immediate admission of Texas into the United States. His opponent, Henry Clay, candidate of the Whig party, came out against immediate admission.

President Tyler interpreted the election victory of Polk as a mandate for the admission of Texas. Since it was clear that the necessary two-thirds vote could not be obtained in the Senate, Tyler found another way. It was proposed that Texas be admitted by a joint resolution of Congress, which required only a majority vote. Congress acted promptly, passing the resolution early in 1845. On March 1, 1845, only three days before he left office, Tyler signed the resolution and dispatched an agent to Texas to conclude the arrangements. One of the provisions of the resolution was:

New states, of convenient size, not exceeding four in number, in addition to said state of Texas and having sufficient population, may hereafter, by the consent of said state, be formed out of the territory thereof, which shall be entitled to admission under the provisions of the Federal Constitution.

Jackson, who had been working behind the scenes for years to make Texas part of the United States, wrote to Houston:

I congratulate you, I congratulate Texas and the United States. . . . I now behold the great American eagle, with her stars and stripes hovering over the lone star of Texas . . . and proclaiming to Mexico and all foreign governments, "You must not attempt to tread upon Texas." . . . Glorious results! In which you, General, have acted a noble part.

It took nine months to complete the formalities of making Texas part of the United States. Faced with the reality of losing Texas, Mexico made a last-minute attempt to prevent its being absorbed into the colossus to the north. Mexico offered to recognize Texan independence. The Texans had a firm offer from the United States, however, and on July 4, 1845, accepted it. The final papers were signed on December 29, 1845, and Texas was formally admitted into the union as the twenty-eighth state. In the state capitol in Austin on February 16, 1846, the Lone Star flag was lowered, ending the nine-year existence of the Texas Republic. That flag was given to Sam Houston.

Today the state of Texas is smaller than it was then. In 1850 the state sold to the United States for $10 million the northern area, which would eventually encompass parts of New Mexico, Oklahoma, Colorado, Wyoming, and Kansas. That made Texas its present size.

But back in 1846 its southern border was still in dispute. The United States claimed the Rio Grande, and Mexico, not reconciled to the loss of its province, claimed the Nueces River. Relations between the two countries were strained to the breaking point, and war resulted.

8

Oregon

Rained the fore part of the day. I determined to go as far as
St. Charles, a French village seven leagues up the Missouri,
and wait at that place until Captain Lewis could finish the
business in which he was obliged to attend to at St. Louis, and
join me by land from that place 24 miles; by this movement I
calculated that if any alterations in the loading of the vessels
or other changes [were] necessary, that they might be made at
St. Charles.

I set out at 4 o'clock p.m. in the presence of many of the
neighbouring inhabitents and proceeded under a gentle breeze
up the Missouri to the upper point of the first island 4 miles
and camped on the island.

That was part of the first entry in the log of the Lewis and
Clark expedition, perhaps the most famous exploration in the
history of the United States. It was written by Captain William
Clark, one of the coleaders of the expedition, on May 14,
1804. The other leader, Captain Meriwether Lewis, joined
the party a week later, and they were ready to go.

The party consisted of fourteen soldiers, nine volunteers,

mostly Kentucky backwoodsmen, a hunter and interpreter, two French voyageurs, and a servant named York. Their equipment consisted of a keelboat fifty-five feet long, armed with two heavy swivel guns fore and aft, and two smaller boats. These carried seven bales of clothing and supplies, sixty tons of food, and fourteen bales of Indian trade goods, including needles, fishhooks, tobacco, knives, silk ribbon, and beads.

They had these instructions from President Jefferson: "The object of your mission is to explore the Missouri River, & such principal streams of it, as, by its course & communication with the waters of the Pacific Ocean, may offer the most direct and practicable water communications across this continent, for the purposes of trade."

Thus their goal was to find the Northwest Passage that explorers of many nations for three hundred years had sought in vain. The Missouri River was the last hope of discovering a quick and easy passage between the oceans. There were two prizes at stake: the vast no-man's-land extending westward from the Mississippi and claimed by England, Spain, Russia, and the United States; and the rich fur trade, the great wealth of the beaver along the inland waterways and of the sea otter on the Pacific coast.

The two men Jefferson selected to command the expedition were young but seasoned army officers. Meriwether Lewis was twenty-nine, a captain of infantry and a former secretary to Jefferson. An introspective man, he had a restless, scientific, thoughtful mind. His companion, William Clark, was thirty-three, a lieutenant in the artillery. Lewis called him captain and made him an equal in command. He was a perfect complement to Lewis, an extrovert, deeply interested in people, with a genius for talking to Indians.

Clark noted in his diary on May 21:

Set out at half passed three o'clock under three cheers from the gentlemen on the bank and proceeded on to the head of the island, which is situated on the stbd [starboard] side, 3 miles.

During the rest of May and June they made their way up the Missouri River in its easiest stretches. They faced squalls, rain, and humid heat. They learned about sandbars, ticks, and mosquitoes. They took voluminous notes, a practice they were to continue throughout the trip. Clark did most of the mapping of the land, while Lewis walked on the riverbank frequently, gathering data on the topography, wildlife, and plants.

On July 21, sixty-nine days out, they reached the mouth of the Platte River (in Nebraska) and met Indians for the first time. They pushed ahead, and on August 20 one of their sergeants, Charles Floyd, died, apparently of a ruptured appendix, and was buried by the river's side. He was the only member of the expedition to lose his life. On September 5 they caught their first glimpse of an antelope (in South Dakota). They were in the heart of the buffalo country, eating well and enjoying buffalo steaks.

On the morning of September 25 they ran into difficulties with Indians (near what is now Pierre, South Dakota). This was the land of the Teton Sioux, who made it a practice to levy tribute on passersby, to rob traders, and to make war on their neighbors. If the Americans wanted to go farther upriver, they would have to leave behind one of their boats with all its goods, the Indians said. Lewis and Clark refused. When the Indians attempted to seize one of the boats, Lewis orderd the swivel guns trained on the shore. The Indians vastly outnumbered the white men and could have wiped them out, but they would have had to pay a heavy price in dead and wounded. They backed down, and the expedition continued.

Charles Willson Peale's portraits of William Clark (*left*) and Meriwether Lewis. *Independence National Historical Park Collection.*

They reached the first of their principal geographic goals,
the Mandan towns near the mouth of the Knife River (north
of Bismarck, North Dakota), on October 27. They had been
on the Missouri for twenty-three weeks and had traveled sixteen hundred miles. Here they set up winter quarters, to
prepare for the big push to the western ocean in the spring.
Here too they saw traces of the Canadian fur traders who
worked in the vicinity. At the fort they hired an interpreter,
Toussaint Charbonneau, who would accompany them in the
spring, bringing along his Indian wife, Sacajawea.

On April 7, 1805, they were ready to go. Lewis noted in
his journal:

Our vessels consisted of six small canoes and two large pirogues.
This little fleet, although not so respectable as that of Columbus

or Captain Cook, was still viewed by us with as much pleasure
as those deservedly famed adventurers ever beheld theirs, and,
I daresay, with quite as much anxiety for their safety and preservation. We were now about to penetrate a country at least
two thousand miles in width, on which the foot of civilized man
had never trod. The good or evil it had in store for us was for
experiment yet to determine, and these little vessels contained
every article by which we were to expect to subsist or defend
ourselves. However, as the state of mind in which we are generally gives coloring to events, when the imagination is suffered
to wander into futurity, the picture which now presented itself
to me was a most pleasing one.

Moving steadily up the Missouri River, in territories unknown to white men, the expedition made discoveries daily.
On April 25 they reached the Yellowstone River; on April 29
they saw a grizzly bear; on May 8 they arrived at the Milk
River; on May 20, the Musselshell River. Well into Montana,
they caught a glimpse of snow-covered mountains far to the
west, on May 26.

On June 3 they reached the junction of two large rivers and
had to decide which one to follow. Despite the advice of their
interpreter, they decided that the southern river was the true
mountain river and continued on it. On June 12 they arrived
at the great falls of the Missouri, vindicating their judgment.
But they faced a serious problem: How to get around the
seventeen miles of rushing water tumbling over five falls and
a series of rapids?

They built crude wagons, using the mast of one of the small
boats for axles. It was hard work, made harder by the heat
and the danger of rattlesnakes. On July 4 the portage was
completed and the men celebrated by drinking the last of the
whiskey they had brought. Far behind their schedule, they

resumed their journey in their fleet of canoes, augmented by two more they built on the way. They arrived at the three forks of the Missouri (now Three Forks, Montana) on July 17. This was the spot where Sacajawea had been taken prisoner five years before. They named the three rivers the Jefferson, the Madison, and the Gallatin.

For four months now, the expedition had traversed the rugged land and not seen a single Indian. Lewis, worried, wrote in his diary:

> We begin to feel considerable anxiety with respect to the Snake Indians. If we do not find them or some other nation who have horses, I fear the successful issue of our voyage will be very doubtful, or at all events, much more difficult in its accomplishment. We are now several hundred miles within the bosom of this wild and mountainous country, where game may rationally be expected to become scarce and subsistence precarious without any information with respect to the country, not knowing how far these mountains continue, or where to direct our course to pass them to advantage or intercept a navigable branch of the Columbia; or even if we were on such a one, the probability is that we should not find any timber within these mountains large enough for canoes, if we judge from the portion of them through which we have passed.
>
> However, I still hope for the best and intend taking a tramp myself in a few days to find these yellow gentlemen [Indians] if possible.

The expedition had traversed the Missouri River from beginning to end and now chose one of its three sources, the most northerly, the Jefferson River. As they labored up the Jefferson, they came to the conclusion that the Northwest Passage they and others had sought for three centuries was a dream. There was no easy passage between the rivers that

In 1905 Charles M. Russell painted this scene in which (*in canoe at right*) Meriwether Lewis stands beside Sacajawea as she addresses an approaching Chinook Indian party. *Amon Carter Museum, Fort Worth.*

flowed east to the Mississippi and those that flowed west to the Columbia. The mountain rivers were too swift, narrow, and shallow for anything but a towrope.

It was in this area that Sacajawea proved most helpful. On August 8 she recognized a rock called Beaver Head (about twelve miles south of Twin Bridges, Montana) and said her people lived on the river to the west. Lewis, with three other men, decided to cross the country by land until they found the Indians. On August 11 they saw an Indian in the distance. On the following day they went through Lemhi Pass (near

Dillon, Montana) and found a stream flowing west. They had crossed the Continental Divide, the first Americans ever to do so.

The next day, August 13, Lewis met some Indians who were friendly but suspicious. Five days later Clark and the rest of the party, including Sacajawea, arrived. The meeting between the Indian woman and her people was dramatic. She ran forward, sucking her fingers to indicate that she had recognized the members of her tribe. It was the same band of Shoshones from which she had been captured five years earlier. By an incredible coincidence, Cameahwait, its chief, was her brother.

Now helpful, the Indians gave Lewis and Clark practical advice: There was no waterway west from the headwaters of the Missouri to any navigable tributary of the Columbia. They did say, however, that a tribe of Indians, the Nez Percé, who lived on the far side of the Rockies, sometimes came east to hunt buffalo on the Great Plains; thus a trail existed. The Shoshones furnished horses so that the white men could follow that trail.

On the morning of August 30 the expedition broke camp and headed north. Then began one of the most difficult parts of the venture. They crossed and recrossed the Continental Divide; their horses slipped and fell over "some of the worst roads that horses ever passed." It rained and it snowed. They were hungry, wet, and miserable as they worked their way up the Bitterroot Valley, always with high, snowcapped mountains to the west, blocking their way.

On September 8 they reached a creek flowing from the west, and they camped to rest a day there (just south of Missoula, Montana). Turning west, the men followed the Nez Percé trail for nine more days. The trail hugged the high mountain ridges, at times above the clouds. There was no

game in sight; the men ate dried food. The horses slipped
and fell. For the first time the men's morale was low.

On September 18 Clark wrote in his diary:

> A fair morning. Cold. I proceeded on in advance with six hunt-
> ers. Made 32 miles and encamped on a bold running creek
> passing to the left, which I call Hungry Creek, as at that place
> we had nothing to eat.

Two days later the expedition broke out of the rugged
mountains and met the Nez Percé, only a few miles from the
Clearwater River (near Greer, Idaho). The ordeal of the mountains was over. The men ate salmon from the Columbia River
and promptly got dysentery. Weak as they were, they went
to work, however, and made dugout canoes out of pine.

From then on, it was clear sailing. On October 7 they went
down the Clearwater River, and by October 10 they had
entered the Snake River (on the border of Idaho and
Washington—the cities of Lewiston, Idaho, and Clarkston,
Washington, mark the river junction). On October 16 they
entered the Columbia River and proceeded downstream,
bypassing the rapids without too much difficulty. On November 6, 1805, Clark entered in his journal:

> Great joy in camp. We are in view of the ocean, this great
> Pacific Ocean which we have been so long anxious to see, and
> the roaring or noise made by the waves breaking on the rocky
> shores (as I suppose) may be heard distinctly.

Actually Clark was a little premature. They had heard the
waves breaking on the estuary of the Columbia. It was seven
days before they reached the Pacific, thus completing the
major part of their mission. On December 3 Clark carved the
following message on a large pine tree on the coast:

Capt. William Clark December 3d 1805. By Land.
U.States in 1804–1805

Later that month they established their winter quarters on the south bank of the Columbia, where it joins the ocean, and called their camp Fort Clatsop (after an Indian tribe in the area).

Lewis and Clark were not the first white men to reach the mouth of the Columbia, however. Almost twenty years earlier, only thirteen days after the Constitution of the United States was approved, the ship *Columbia*, commanded by Captain Robert Gray, cleared Boston harbor. It sailed around Cape Horn and then up the coast to Vancouver Island, where the crew traded iron tools, looking glasses, and beads for the skin of sea otter. Then across the wide Pacific to Canton, China, where Gray exchanged the skins, in great demand by Chinese mandarins, for tea, porcelain, silk, and cotton cloth, in equally great demand on his return to Boston. It was a highly profitable business, based on the fur of the sea otter.

Captain Gray made a second trip, in 1792, three hundred years after Columbus. On May 12 he discovered a spacious harbor. His log recorded:

> At four a.m. saw entrance of our desired port bearing east-southeast, distance six leagues; in steering sails, and hauled our wind in shore. At eight a.m., being a little to windward of the harbor, bore away, and ran in east-north-east between the breakers, having from five to seven fathoms of water. When we were over the bar, we found this to be a large river of fresh water, up which we steered.

Captain Gray had discovered the mighty river that now bears the name of his ship, and he firmly established United States claims to the Northwest. But he was not the only explorer on the Pacific coast that year. At sea, earlier, Gray had

met His Majesty's ships *Discovery* and *Chatham*, commanded
by Captain George Vancouver and Lieutenant William R.
Broughton. Vancouver sailed north and made the first entrance into Puget Sound, which was named after one of his
lieutenants, and sailed around the large island that now bears
his name. Sailing south, he detached Broughton to check
Gray's findings. Broughton sailed up the Columbia for almost
a hundred miles, decided that Gray had not actually entered
the river, and claimed for Britain the river and its watershed.
Thus two rival claims to the area were established. (Spain and
Russia too believed they had rights established by exploration
on the Pacific coast.)

A few years earlier, in 1789, a young Canadian of Scottish
descent, Alexander Mackenzie, an employee of the North
West Company, had begun the first two explorations that
solidified British claims to the vast northwestern area of North
America. Starting from the farthest western outpost of white
civilization, Fort Chipewyan on the western end of Lake
Athabasca in Canada, in yellow birch canoes he went up the
Slave River to Great Slave Lake and then down a large river
that flowed westward. He thought he had reached a waterway
to the Pacific, but the river turned north into the bare countryside of the Arctic, so desolate that no game for food was
available.

Mackenzie persevered and on July 17, 1789, he reached
salt water, the Arctic Ocean, instead of the warm Pacific. He
named the river the Disappointment, but later it was renamed
after him. The Mackenzie is the second longest river in North
America.

Four years later, in 1792, as Robert Gray was exploring the
coast of the Northwest, Mackenzie set off by land to reach
the same area. This time the Peace River that flowed east into
Lake Athabasca was the route. Mackenzie and his party spent

the winter at the junction of the Smoky and Peace Rivers and on May 9, 1793, set off again into the wild unknown in birch-bark canoes. Six days later they saw the snowcapped Rockies for the first time. Four days farther on they entered the Peace River Canyon but were unable to cope with the raging mountain river. They towed the canoe with lines; they portaged frequently. After six days of incredible turmoil and danger, they finally conquered the river by bypassing it. They came to the Parsnip River, found some friendly Indians, and finally reached a river flowing west, the Bad River. Once again their canoes were tossed about and overturned; they lost their gear, food, and ammunition.

But Mackenzie was determined that nothing would stop him. He pushed his grumbling men on till they reached the Blackwater River and a trail the Indians said would lead to the sea. With hundred-pound packs on their backs, the men set off by land, and on July 16 reached the Bella Coola River, flowing west. There Indians took them in their own canoes and shot the rapids. On July 20, 1793, they reached a wide and rocky inlet and saw seals, porpoises, and gulls. They had reached the Pacific, about a hundred miles north of Vancouver. Mackenzie marked a rock:

Alexander Mackenzie, from Canada by land,
the twenty-second of July, 1793

Mackenzie was the first white man to cross North America by land. He had fulfilled the dream of explorers of many nations who had come to the New World after Columbus to seek a Northwest Passage to the Indies and to riches. He had done it in the name of the North West Company, which had been organized to tap the fur trade of northern North America.

In a book about his explorations, *Voyages from Montreal,* he outlined his plans for a continental fur trade, to be operated, of course, by the British. The key to his plan was the Columbia River, which he insisted must be British. "By opening this intercourse between the Atlantic and Pacific Oceans," he wrote, "and forming regular establishments through the interior and both extremes, as well as along the coasts and islands, the entire command of the fur trade of North America might be obtained."

One of his most attentive readers was Thomas Jefferson, and Mackenzie's book was one of the reasons for the Lewis and Clark expedition. Immediately after that expedition returned to St. Louis, in September 1806, Lewis wrote to Jefferson that the country between the Missouri and the Rocky Mountains "is richer in beaver and otter than any country on earth." These furs could be shipped along the inland route to the mouth of the Columbia and then transshipped on ocean-going vessels to reach Canton "earlier than the furs which are annually shipped from Montreal arrive in England." The Americans too were well aware of the economic consequences of their discoveries.

There immediately followed a race for the fur riches of the Northwest. The Canadians Simon Fraser and David Thompson, of the North West Company, were already in the area, scouting routes, trying to find their way to the Columbia. Fraser in 1808 found instead the river that bears his name and flows into the Strait of Georgia, too far north to be commercially useful. But he and Thompson by 1810 had established several trading posts on the western slopes of the Rockies.

In that same year an American fur merchant, John Jacob Astor, entered the picture by creating the American Fur Company. He had a vision of monopolizing the trade by establishing a post at the mouth of the Columbia. He sent his ship the *Tonquin* from New York in September 1810, and it arrived at the Columbia in April 1811. His men established themselves not far from where Fort Clatsop had been built and called their settlement Astoria. They beat Thompson to the mouth of the Columbia by about four months; he arrived there on July 15 and found the American flag flying.

Astor's overland expedition to supply Astoria had much more difficulty. It was beset by the same kind of problems as were faced by Lewis and Clark: bad weather, hostile Indians, loss of food, wrong directions, overturned canoes, Rocky Mountain storms, near-starvation. These pioneers struggled into Astoria in January and February 1812.

It was an unfortunate year for Astor's design. The war that broke out far to the east between England and the United States spelled the ruin of his venture. His aides in Astoria sold out to the powerful North West Company at tremendous financial loss to Astor. Further, a British warship arrived there on November 30, 1812, took possession of Fort Astoria, and raised the British flag. Astor had failed in his business enterprise, but he had established another American claim to the Columbia, a claim that was never relinquished.

The Treaty of Ghent, at the end of the War of 1812, provided that each side would restore captured possessions. Secretary of State James Monroe notified the British of United States intentions to reoccupy the Columbia River outpost. The British, at the insistence of the North West Company, delayed. Two years later Monroe, now president of the United States, ordered the USS *Ontario* to take possession of the region. Under the pressure of this threat, the British yielded. On August 19, 1818, the *Ontario*, under the command of Captain James Biddle, once more raised the American flag at Astoria. A large board was painted, proclaiming:

Taken possession of in the name
and on the behalf of the
United States
by Captain James Biddle, commanding the
United States sloop of war Ontario
Columbia River, August 1818

In the same year, United States and British representatives were meeting (see Chapter 7) on the border between Canada and the United States. They agreed that the forty-ninth parallel would be the border to the Rocky Mountains. The area between the mountains and the ocean would be "free and open for the term of ten years . . . to the Vessels, Citizens and Subjects of the two Powers," without prejudice to either. In effect, both countries agreed to let the dispute simmer.

Secretary of State John Quincy Adams also had to settle the claims of two other nations to the area. In the protracted discussions that led to the Adams–de Onís Treaty of 1819, Spain agreed to a boundary of forty-two degrees north latitude from the Rocky Mountains to the Pacific Ocean as the limit of the Spanish possessions in the southwest. This line is the present northern boundary of California and Nevada. Then Adams turned his attention to Russia, which had colonized Alaska and had sent ships down the coast as far as California. She too had claims in the Pacific Northwest.

He proposed to the Russians a ten-year treaty allowing each nation freedom of navigation and trade on the coast. He further proposed that no American citizen would make settlement north of the fifty-fifth parallel, nor would Russian subjects move south of that line.

Adams had in mind a boundary line between the United States and Canada at the fifty-first parallel and thought that his proposal would allow each of the three nations concerned ample room for colonization and trade. In St. Petersburg, the Russians had no serious objections to the American proposals. The only modification was drawing the line at 54°40', so that the entire Prince of Wales Island would be left within the Russian sphere. To this the Americans quickly agreed, and in April 1824 an agreement was signed.

Now the disputed Oregon territory concerned the United States and Britain only. Several times in the following years the two parties attempted to settle the dispute, but the key differences remained. The British wanted the boundary to be on the Columbia River and rejected an offer by the United States to accept a continuation of the forty-ninth parallel line. The United States held out for that line and as a bargaining device insisted that the fifty-first parallel was its objective. Several times in the 1820s a bill to extend United States law to American citizens in Oregon was rejected by Congress as likely to lead to a military collision with Britain. The compromise of 1818, leaving the area open to both countries, was extended several times.

The Americans had beaten the British to the Columbia, but the British poured men and supplies into the region. The bastion of the British occupation was Fort Vancouver on the north bank of the Columbia River, about six miles north of where the Willamette River flows in. It was operated by the Hudson's Bay Company, which in 1821 had absorbed the North West Company. The man who ran it, John McLoughlin—born in Canada in 1784 and educated as a doctor in Paris but converted to the fur business—became the ruler of the Northwest. His official rank was chief factor; his subordinates called him governor; the Indians gave him the name "White-Headed Eagle."

From Fort Vancouver, McLoughlin sent out brigades in all directions to gather in furs, the chief business of his company.

He encouraged small farmers in the immediate area of the fort and was regarded by all as an enlightened monarch. The Hudson's Bay Company ruled the area, and John McLoughlin, an educated man with a heart, was its voice.

As the first Americans came into the region, they were greeted hospitably by McLoughlin. In 1832 Nathaniel J. Wyeth of Boston and a small party arrived in distress. McLoughlin fed them. Wyeth went back east, and then returned, accompanied by Jason Lee and other missionaries. Their trip failed, but they published a book about Oregon that described the beautiful country and the opportunities to be found there.

In 1835 the American Board of Commissioners for Foreign Missions sent out a minister, Samuel Parker, to found missions for the Indians. In 1836 Dr. Marcus Whitman and his twenty-year-old bride, Narcissa, came by covered wagon on the southern route from Fort Laramie to Fort Boise and Walla Walla and then down the Columbia, where McLoughlin welcomed them. After them, Americans came in increasingly large numbers. McLoughlin suggested that they settle in the Willamette Valley to the south of the Columbia River, and most of them did so.

The Americans in 1840 numbered only about one hundred persons, but after that a population boom was on. The reports of Lewis and Clark, then the books of the missionaries and the tales of the explorers, stirred the imagination of Americans.

They started west in astonishing numbers, first to the Mississippi and then, braving Indians and the elements, to the Rockies and beyond. First came the trappers and the mountain men; behind them came the adventurers; then the settlers, some of them with their wives and children.

The frontier beckoned to America, and Americans responded. The lure of the West was irresistible to hundreds of people, then thousands and tens of thousands. No matter that this was Indian land, that the grazing lands of the plains had been guaranteed to the Indians displaced by earlier settlers in the East. Once again the Indians were pushed aside. They fought back, they were betrayed, but the tide of emigration to the West was no more subject to control than the ocean waves.

Tough mountain men found easier routes through passes and trails that wagons could negotiate, thus making it possible for the settlers to make their way. Jedediah Smith, for example, rediscovered South Pass, the most famous gateway across the Continental Divide, in south central Wyoming. It had been discovered much earlier, in 1812, by Robert Stuart, returning from Astoria to New York, but his discovery had been overlooked. South Pass, a series of broad rolling hills, about twenty miles wide, was the key to the overland trail to Oregon (and California).

The trail started at Independence, Missouri, where "prairie schooners," or canvas-covered Conestoga wagons, assembled in the spring for the long trip west. A party consisted of perhaps a hundred such wagons, with a captain in charge and an experienced mountain man as guide, and perhaps a herd of cattle following. The wagons moved up the west bank of the Missouri to Fort Leavenworth in Kansas, the border of Indian, and unknown, territory. There were no roads from then on. The wagons moved slowly to Council Bluffs, then west along the Platte River and through the Great Plains. There were rivers to cross, storms to weather, Indians to fight. It was not easy.

Wagons followed the north fork of the Platte River to Fort Laramie (Wyoming), where the mountains began. Next came the long trek to South Pass and thus over the Continental

Divide down to Fort Bridger in the southwestern corner of Wyoming. The trail then moved them northwesterly into Idaho to Fort Hall on the Snake River. The next objective was Fort Boise, and then Fort Walla Walla on the Columbia. The wagons went down the southern bank of the Columbia until they reached the Fort Vancouver area. If the venturesome settlers were lucky, they might reach the end of their trip by Thanksgiving Day, six months after they started.

The first political convention of Americans in Oregon met in 1843, near what is now Salem, and chose three commissioners to govern them. In 1845 a constitution was adopted and a governor appointed. All this was done over the objections of the British, who believed that they had equal rights in Oregon. The problem of who owned Oregon was becoming more and more important. It was up to the politicians and diplomats in Washington and London to find a solution.

On May 27, 1844, the Democratic National Convention met in Baltimore. The atmosphere was heavy with suspicion and distrust. Martin Van Buren, who had been president of the United States from 1837 to 1841, came into the convention with more than half the delegates pledged to nominate him for the presidency once again. But there was a growing opposition to him from Southern delegates alienated by his stand against the annexation of Texas. In the first act of the convention, these delegates and those who favored other candidates adopted a two-thirds rule; that is, a vote of two-thirds of the delgates would be required to nominate a candidate.

On the first ballot Van Buren received a majority of the votes, as had been expected—146 of a total of 266. From then on, it was downhill for Van Buren. On the seventh and last ballot on the first day of the convention, his total dropped to 99. There were three other candidates in the running, but none of them sparked any enthusiasm. Behind the scenes,

Democratic leaders conferred and bargained far into the night.

The next morning George Bancroft of Massachusetts arose and nominated a man whose name had not even been mentioned the previous day. He was James Knox Polk, former Speaker of the House of Representatives. On the eighth ballot Polk received forty-four votes. On the ninth ballot the convention stampeded to his standard and he was nominated unanimously—the first dark horse in American political history, a man who had not even been considered for the nomination before the convention opened.

Polk was not without credentials, however. Born in North Carolina in 1795, he had received a law degree from the University of North Carolina and had migrated to Tennessee and served as a representative from that state from 1825 to 1839. In Washington he was such a firm supporter of President Jackson that he was sometimes called "Young Hickory," an obvious allusion to Jackson's nickname, "Old Hickory." In 1839 Polk had been elected governor of Tennessee but had been defeated for reelection. The key point in his favor was that he was supported by Jackson and that he was an ardent expansionist.

Like most of his countrymen, he believed that the United States was destined to expand from sea to sea. He, and they, believed in "manifest destiny," the idea that the expansion of the United States was the wave of the future. Polk's platform called for the reoccupation of Oregon and the reoccupation of Texas. ("Reoccupation" referred to his belief that these lands truly belonged to the United States by previous treaties.)

Polk's opponent for the presidency was Henry Clay, undisputed leader of the Whig party and a power in Congress for years. Clay opposed the expansion of the United States into Texas. His platform did not even mention the issue, a clear misreading of the temper of the country. Polk won the election and on his inaugural day was confronted with two crises.

One, with Britain, concerned Oregon in the northwest. The other, with Mexico, concerned Texas in the southwest. On the Texas issue, Polk endorsed the steps taken by his predecessor to annex the region. On Oregon, he had this to say in his inaugural address on March 4, 1845:

> Nor will it become in a less degree my duty to assert and maintain by all constitutional means the right of the United States to that portion of our territory which lies beyond the Rocky Mountains. Our title to the country of Oregon is clear and unquestionable, and already our people are preparing to perfect that title by occupying it with their wives and children.

In July the State Department sent a note to the British laying claim to the whole of the Oregon territory up to the 54° 40' line that Adams many years before had set as the southern limit of the Russian claims. It was at about this time that the cry was being heard around the country: "Fifty-four–forty, or fight!"

Secretary of State James Buchanan, acting on Polk's instructions, offered to settle the question by accepting the forty-ninth degree as the border, but the British ambassador rejected this proposal. Polk decided to use American public opinion, as expressed by the fighting slogan, to force the British to settle. In his first annual message to Congress, early in 1846, he restated the American claim to the whole of the Oregon territory and requested Congress to abrogate the treaty with Britain providing for joint occupation of the area. Privately he advised the American envoy in London that if the British government offered to settle on the forty-nine-degree line, he would feel obligated to bring that proposal before Congress.

The carrot-and-the-stick technique worked. Congress acted on Polk's suggestion that the treaty for joint occupancy be terminated. When the British learned of this, they offered to accept the forty-nine-degree line. On June 10, 1846, Polk submitted the British offer to the Senate, and two days later it was accepted by a vote of thirty-seven to twelve. The treaty signed by the president on June 19 provided the following:

> From the point on the forty-ninth parallel of North latitude, where the boundary laid down in existing treaties and conventions between the United States and Great Britain terminates, the line between the territories of the United States and those of His Britannic Majesty shall continue westward along the said forty-ninth parallel of north latitude to the middle of the channel which separates the continent from Vancouver's Island; and thence southerly through the middle of said Channel, and of Fuca's Straits to the Pacific Ocean.

Polk had extricated himself from the danger of conflict on two fronts, the northwest and the southwest. Oregon was now part of the United States, and the settlement came just in time. The United States was involved in a war in the southwest.

9

California

IN MAY 1846 THE UNITED STATES declared war on Mexico. Colonel Stephen W. Kearny, commanding the First Dragoons in Fort Leavenworth on the Missouri River, received orders from the War Department that same month. He was to organize an Army of the West to conquer New Mexico, then a Mexican province; next he was to organize a government for the United States there; and then, if he could, he was to proceed westward and conquer California.

On the map back in Washington it might have looked easy. The map showed only distances; it did not show desert, rattlesnakes, thirst, mountains, or Indians. An experienced officer, one who had explored and traveled the expanse of the West, Kearny set about organizing his forces and supplies. On June 29 he was ready. With sixteen hundred men and sixteen cannons, Kearny, newly promoted to the rank of brigadier general, left Fort Leavenworth. His first stop: Santa Fe, capital of New Mexico. His real destination: California.

The vision of golden California as part of the United States was the real cause of the Mexican War. There were tensions on the Mexican border, there were problems concerning the annexation of Texas, there were insults and misunderstandings on both sides—all this was true enough. But behind the hostile attitudes and moves was the fact that the United States was determined to expand to the Pacific. Neither Indians nor the elements nor the legality of Mexican claims was going to stand in the way. Manifest destiny was in the air Americans breathed, and President Polk was determined to do all in his power to stretch the geographical limits of the United States to the Pacific Ocean. Polk did not want war, he merely wanted the fruits of war, the land and territory of a neighboring country.

President Tyler interpreted the election of Polk as a mandate to annex Texas and, even before Polk took office, signed a joint resolution of Congress proclaiming the annexation. Then he sent a mission to Texas to effect the merger, whereupon the Mexican ambassador to the United States demanded his passport, a step generally regarded as a rupture in relations between nations. The ambassador immediately returned to Mexico. Thus, on the day he assumed office, Polk faced a critical decision. His decision was to endorse the moves taken by his predecessor and to make it clear that he would do all in his power to help the United States expand.

At about the time that Polk assumed the presidency, Mexico too had a new president. The dictator Santa Anna had been deposed and exiled to Cuba. Like Polk, the new Mexican president, José Joaquín Herrera, said he wanted peace. The specific differences at dispute then were two: United States financial claims against the Mexican government, a minor issue; and the major issue, the conflict over the border between Texas and Mexico. The United States claimed the Rio Grande as the border; Mexico claimed that the boundary of Texas historically had never extended beyond the Nueces

River. In August 1845 it appeared that the two nations, despite the diplomatic break, would be willing to talk about their differences.

Polk decided to send John Slidell (who was to become famous later as a Confederate agent) to Mexico with instructions to clear up the claims question and to settle the border dispute. His intentions were much broader in scope, however. Polk confided in his diary, which he wrote in the third person:

> One great object of the mission, as stated by the President, would be to adjust a permanent boundary between the United States and Mexico, and that in doing this the Minister would be instructed to purchase for a pecuniary consideration Upper California and New Mexico. . . . The President said that for such a boundary the amount of pecuniary consideration to be paid would be of small importance. He supposed it might be had for fifteen or twenty millions, but he was ready to pay forty millions for it, if it could not be had for less.

Polk also took certain military steps, in case the negotiations failed. In August 1845 he ordered General Zachary Taylor, in command of the Army of the Southwest, to move to Corpus Christi on the Nueces River and await further orders there. He also ordered warships from the Pacific and Gulf squadrons to positions nearer the Mexican coast. The senior United States naval officer in the Pacific, Commander John D. Sloat, already had orders to seize California if war broke out.

While these military moves were taking place, Slidell arrived in Mexico City. He found the Mexican government in a panic. Mexican public opinion at that time viewed the United States as aggressive, cruel, greedy. The mere arrival of Slidell brought criticisms of Herrera as weak and treacherous. Cries of "national honor" were sounded in the press of Mexico.

Under the circumstances the Mexican president was help-less. He wanted peace, and he knew that Mexico could not wage a successful war against the United States. If he rec-ognized Slidell, however, he would be giving in to the American demands, thus bringing his own downfall. To refuse would probably mean war. Herrera did what any politician would do: He temporized.

As 1846 dawned, the Americans began to grow impatient. Polk ordered a naval force to take up positions outside Vera Cruz. In March he instructed Taylor to move his army to the Rio Grande, taking possession of the disputed area between the Nueces and the Rio Grande. In Mexico City the obtuse American envoy Slidell, who could not see the Mexican di-lemma, demanded recognition or his passport. He received his passport.

When Polk heard the news, he determined to gain by force what he could not win by diplomacy. On May 9 he told his cabinet that "in my opinion we had ample cause of war and that it was impossible that we could stand in status quo or that I could remain silent much longer." Only one member of the cabinet dissented from his decision to send a war mes-sage to Congress. He was George Bancroft, secretary of the navy. Bancroft agreed, however, that if any act of hostility were committed by Mexican forces, he too would be in favor of immediate war.

At six o'clock on the evening of May 9, a dispatch from Taylor arrived in Washington. He reported that on April 24, on the east side of the Rio Grande, he had been attacked by Mexican troops and several Americans had been killed. The cabinet promptly reconvened and unanimously approved of war. Polk told Congress that the Mexicans "have at last in-vaded our territory and shed the blood of our fellow-citizens on our own soil." He described the action as follows:

The Mexican forces at Matamoros assumed a belligerent attitude, and on the 12th of April General Ampudia, then in command, notified General Taylor to break up his camp within twenty-four hours and to retire to the Nueces River and in the event of his failure to comply with these demands announced that arms, and arms alone, must decide the question. But no open act of hostility was committed until the 24th day of April. On that day, General Arista, who had succeeded to the command of the Mexican forces, communicated to General Taylor that "he considered hostilities commenced and should prosecute them." A party of dragoons of sixty-three men and officers were on the same day dispatched from the American camp up the Rio Grande del Norte, on its left bank, to ascertain whether the Mexican troops had crossed or were preparing to cross the river, and became engaged with a large body of these troops and after a short affair, in which some sixteen were killed or wounded, appear to have been surrounded and compelled to surrender.

As war exists, and, notwithstanding all our efforts to avoid it, exists by the act of Mexico herself, we are called upon by every consideration of duty and patriotism to vindicate with decision the honor, the rights and the interests of our country. . . . I invoke the prompt action of Congress to recognize the existence of war.

That evening Secretary of State James Buchanan proposed to send a letter to American ministers abroad, containing this sentence: "In going to war, we do not do so with a view to acquire either California or New Mexico or any other portion of Mexican territory." Polk ordered the sentence deleted. Coldly realistic, he knew that California was the prize he sought. Congress, as could be expected, backed the president and voted a declaration of war.

There were three American forces in the field. General

Taylor commanded the main striking force in a war that Polk hoped would be quick and easy. General John E. Wool headed another force farther north, whose objective was to move toward Chihuahua. Farther north still was General Kearny and his dragoons, augmented by large numbers of volunteers.

Kearny's force moved swiftly on the Santa Fe Trail, a well-traveled road through the plains. The sun was hot, hotter than on the farms most of his volunteers came from. Hundreds of rattlesnakes were killed on the march. Mosquitoes were constant companions. One of the daily chores was gathering buffalo chips for fuel; there were no trees or firewood on the dusty plains. The men saw herds of buffalo and killed some of them for food. They finally reached Bent's Fort, a landmark in the West, where the trail curved down through the mountains to Santa Fe. Kearny had lost most of his horses to the heat and the elements. His food supply was dwindling; he cut rations in half.

On August 1 he started out again for Santa Fe. The heat was intense, the sun hotter than the men could believe possible. For four days they marched through lands so arid that there was no grass at all for the horses. Wolves trotted near the column of marchers, waiting for horses to drop. The men got dysentery from the alkali water in the few holes they found. Some died from the heat or from disease. But most of them plodded onward until the army reached the mountains and cool, refreshing streams.

On August 18 before dawn Kearny's army marched onto the plains before Santa Fe, prepared for battle. But the Mexican commander, a general in name only, was not prepared to fight. In the late afternoon Kearny rode in front of his troops into the narrow streets of Santa Fe, to the Plaza of the Constitution, the central square. Without firing a shot, he had conquered the Mexican province of New Mexico, as ordered. The American flag was raised and Kearny proclaimed all of New Mexico to be United States territory.

Next he organized a government for New Mexico. He then divided his forces in two. The major part, all of the volunteers, were put into one force and ordered south to invade Mexico, joining up with General Wool at Chihuahua. The other force, three hundred dragoons, he commanded himself. On September 25 they rode out of Santa Fe—for California.

A short while out, on October 6, they met a rider coming east from California. He was Kit Carson, the famous scout, carrying news to Washington that California had been conquered.

Americans in the Sacramento Valley had on June 14 captured Sonoma, the northernmost Mexican settlement in California, and had raised a flag with a crude drawing of a grizzly bear on it. They proclaimed the independent republic of California. Later that same month, news of the outbreak of the war with Mexico reached California and Commander Sloat promptly obeyed orders. His naval forces occupied the coastal cities, meeting little resistance.

The American flag was raised over Monterey on July 7, with a proclamation that "henceforth California will be a portion of the United States." A few days later the bear flag was lowered in Sonoma, ending the short-lived republic, and the United States flag was raised in its place. It seemed that Kearny's work had been done for him.

Carson told him that the terrain ahead was most difficult and that he would not get his wagons through in less than six months. Kearny therefore sent all his wagons back to Santa Fe, along with two hundred dragoons. He sent another dispatch rider east and kept Carson as his guide for the trip to

The U.S. Marines raise the American flag at Monterey, California, in July 1846. Commodore John D. Sloat's Pacific squadron fires a salute. *U.S. Marine Corps Museum.*

California. A hundred men certainly would be enough for an occupation force in conquered California. Once more, Kearny set off for the golden province a thousand miles away.

His hundred men were mounted on mules, which in the desert were better than horses. They also had several pack animals with them. Riding slowly through deep, narrow canyons, pulling two cannons that Kearny insisted on taking along, they reached the upper Gila River in New Mexico on October 20. As they moved down the Gila, one of the men recorded his impressions:

> Every bush in this country is full of thorns—and every piece of grass so soon as it is broken becomes a thorn on both ends—

every rock you turn over has a tarantula or a centipede under
it, and Carson says in the summer the most beautiful specimens
of rattlesnake are scattered in the greatest profusion. . . . The
fact is, take the country altogether, and I defy any man who
has not seen it—or one as utterly worthless—even to imagine
any so barren. The cactus is the only thing that does grow.

On November 22 the army reached the junction of the Gila
with the Colorado River (near Yuma, where today's border
between Arizona and California lies). Having captured some
enemy mail, Kearny had a shock. The Californians had routed
American soldiers and sailors, the Mexican flag flew once more
from San Diego north, the Mexicans were advancing and the
Americans were falling back.

And here he was, a desert to cross and a war to be fought
at the other end, with only a hundred weary soldiers, a mere
one-third of his fighting force—all because of the premature
news that the fighting was over. The hardest part of the journey was ahead, another desert. Kearny's men, tempered by
the heat and by the trials of the early part of the trip, made
it, despite the furious sun and their lack of water. On
December 2 they emerged from the desert onto more fertile
territory—at the point of collapse—and struggled to Warner's
Ranch, the end of the Gila Trail.

A small group of sailors from the American naval force
joined Kearny, and they started on the road to San Diego,
which was blocked by a small body of Californians at San
Pascual. On December 6 the Americans rashly attacked; they
were tired, hungry, soaked through from a night of rain. The
Californians, with fresh horses and dry ammunition, fought
back. They killed eighteen of the attackers and wounded many
more, including Kearny. It was a military defeat for Kearny,
but the Californians failed to press their advantage; he was

able, after a rest, to move ahead to San Diego, and arrived there on December 12.

He found a political shambles. Commodore Robert F. Stockton, an ambitious man, had replaced Sloat as head of the United States naval forces in California. He regarded himself as the conqueror of California, even though it refused to stay conquered. He would not recognize Kearny's authority, influenced undoubtedly by Captain John C. Frémont, whom he had promised to appoint governor. Frémont, a regular United States Army officer, had come west earlier on an exploration and mapping mission and had stayed to fight and play politics. An adventurer and an opportunist, Frémont was the son-in-law of Senator Thomas Hart Benton, a powerful politician in Washington.

Despite these political differences, Stockton did cooperate with Kearny in the military operations necessary to pacify California. On January 8, 1847, their combined forces routed the Californians at the San Gabriel River. On January 10 they entered Los Angeles unopposed. The Californians fled northward and encountered Frémont moving south. On January 13 the Californians formally surrendered to Frémont, gave up their arms, and were permitted to return to their native Mexico if they so chose. Militarily, California was now American.

What followed was a tragicomedy. Stockton still refused to acknowledge Kearny's authority. He appointed Frémont governor, and Frémont compounded the error by accepting the appointment. He notified General Kearny that he would not obey his orders and appealed to his father-in-law for help.

Kearny, regarded by many as one of the ablest officers in the army, waited. In February a new naval officer arrived, replacing Stockton, and without question accepted Kearny as his superior. Later another army officer arrived with orders confirming Kearny as military and civilian governor of California. Kearny then ordered Frémont to muster his own battalion out of service. After some hesitation, Frémont yielded.

Kearny then began the pacification of California and the organization of its government. He placed it under military control for as long as the war with Mexico lasted. (The next steps were in the future: California was to be admitted to the United States in 1850.) In June, Kearny's work was done, and he started east.

Back in Fort Leavenworth, he ordered Frémont to report to Washington under arrest for a military trial. The court met in Washington in November and a few months later delivered its verdict: Frémont was guilty of mutiny, disobedience, and misconduct, and was ordered dismissed from the military service. Acting under political pressure, Polk reversed the mutiny conviction, released Frémont, and ordered him back to duty. Frémont refused the pardon and resigned from the service.

Thereafter Kearny served his country well but was the target of vituperative attacks by Senator Benton. The man who secured New Mexico and California for the United States did not ever receive the acclaim that was due him, largely because of the calumnies of his political enemies.

The conquest of California and New Mexico was practically complete before the war in the south, against the regular armies of Mexico, really began. The force that Kearny had sent south from Santa Fe in September 1845 performed its duties with a minimum of fuss and feathers.

Colonel Alexander W. Doniphan commanded an undisciplined mob of volunteers, ragged in appearance, contemptuous of authority, but magnificent fighters. They marched south along the upper reaches of the Rio Grande and then through the rough Mexican countryside, routing two superior Mexican forces. They reached their objective, Chihuahua, on March 1, 1847. Military historians consider Doniphan's accomplishment—he moved thirty-five hundred miles from Fort Leavenworth without a secure base at his rear—among the most remarkable in history. At Chihuahua he was supposed to meet the American unit commanded by General Wool, but Wool had been diverted to join Taylor's command.

For months, from June through August 1846, Taylor prepared to march into the heart of Mexico. His enemy was not the Mexican soldier but heat, sickness, inadequate transport. Early in September, with six thousand troops, Taylor marched on Monterrey, his first objective. During September 21, 22, and 23, Americans fought their way into the city against desperate resistance, foot by foot. By the twenty-fourth the Mexicans had had enough, and Taylor accepted an agreement for evacuation by the Mexicans, not unconditional surrender. In so doing, Taylor alienated Polk, who said: "It will only enable the Mexican army to reorganize and recruit so as to make another stand."

Polk was also vexed at the duplicity of Santa Anna. He had permitted Santa Anna to return to Mexico through the American naval blockade after private negotiations by way of an intermediary in which Santa Anna had indicated that if he returned to power he would make concessions agreeable to the United States. Santa Anna returned to Vera Cruz in August 1846 and received a hero's welcome. He was swept back into power and set about to prepare for a determined resistance to the Americans. Because of Polk's mistake, Mexico had its ablest general in command and the war was prolonged.

Polk had other problems as well. He had not been able to

buy a victory (by bribing Santa Anna) and he had not been able to win a quick military victory. He had gained all the land the United States desired—California and New Mexico—by the brilliant peripheral campaign of Kearny. But the Mexicans refused to submit. They rallied to Santa Anna in support of their country in time of invasion.

Polk faced domestic political problems too. Taylor, his commanding general in Mexico, was a Whig and opposed to the Democratic party headed by Polk; and Taylor was obviously preparing to run for the presidency himself. General Winfield Scott, commanding officer of the army in Washington, was also a Whig and a potential presidential candidate, but Scott was a capable military man and he had a plan for winning the war fairly quickly. He proposed to make an amphibious landing at Vera Cruz and then follow the route of the Spanish conquerors to the heart of Mexico, Mexico City.

Reluctantly, Polk approved Scott's plan and charged him with winning the war. Scott was a brilliant man, rather elderly at sixty, and a dandy. He had fought in the War of 1812, he had subdued Indians, he had settled the Maine border crisis (see Chapter 6). He was a shrewd judge of men, talented, cultivated, debonair; in short, the complete opposite of the rough-hewn Taylor. He was also vain and loved to dress up in fancy uniforms. For all that, he was the right man for the job; he was a general who believed that careful preparation was the secret of success in war.

In January 1847 Taylor received orders to subordinate himself to Scott, orders that embittered him. It was also suggested that he fall back and concentrate on Monterrey, while Scott prepared for the invasion. Taylor ignored this advice. Instead he moved deeper into Mexico, with fewer than five thousand men. On February 22, 1847, he established himself in what he thought was an impregnable position in the mountains near

Buena Vista and awaited an attack by Santa Anna, who out-numbered him three to one.

The Mexicans found a way to attack around the edge of Taylor's forces and pushed the Americans back, killing and wounding many. The battle appeared to be lost.

But Taylor, the old Indian fighter, was at his best when fighting. He reorganized his troops and turned them around to face the main Mexican threat. He found a reserve unit, a regiment of Mississippi Rifles commanded by Colonel Jefferson Davis, committed them to the battle, and checked the Mexican advance. Santa Anna then threw in his reserves, but the aroused Americans, vastly outnumbered, pushed them back.

At nightfall the two armies stood almost exactly where they had been when the fighting started. During the night the Mexicans pulled back. The courage of the American fighting man had turned defeat into a victory of sorts and given Taylor, despite his tactical mistakes, a reputation that was to win him the presidency the following year.

The fighting in the north was over, but the war was not. As they had on many other occasions, the Mexicans rallied to fight again. Now it was Scott's turn to try to end the war. With the efficient help of the navy, Scott's army landed on March 9, 1847, on a beach three miles south of Vera Cruz. Using sixty-five "surf boats," an army of thirteen thousand men stormed ashore, followed by artillery, horses, and sup-plies, ready for any kind of resistance—but there was none. Scott moved on to Vera Cruz itself, which he captured on March 29.

As Scott prepared to move inland, Polk appointed an envoy to negotiate a peace treaty as soon as the Mexicans were ready. He was Nicholas P. Trist, chief clerk of the State Department, a lawyer who spoke Spanish—and a reliable Democrat, who

The landing of American troops at Vera Cruz. *Anne S. K. Brown Military Collection, Brown University Library.*

had married the granddaughter of Thomas Jefferson. Trist left for Mexico, and upon his arrival he and Scott immediately disliked and distrusted each other. They carried on necessary communications in a series of acrimonious letters. After two months they finally consulted face to face for the first time, and just as mysteriously as their rift had begun, it ended.

Following the route that Hernando Cortés had taken some three hundred years earlier, Scott set off for Mexico City. His army had been reduced because the term of enlistment of many of the volunteers had expired. He had six thousand now, about half the number of troops he thought necessary. Supplies were cut off for weeks and he was forced to make a virtue of necessity. He cut loose from his lines of communication and lived off the countryside. Despite all of the problems, he had many brilliant assistants, several of whom were to become famous in their own right: Captain Robert E. Lee, Captain George B. McClellan, Lieutenant Ulysses S. Grant.

In six months Scott outmaneuvered and outfought Santa Anna in the mountains between the sea and Mexico City. He arrived at the gates of the city in early September. Between the Americans and the Mexican capital stood Santa Anna with fifteen thousand men, almost three times the strength of Scott's army.

The Battle of Chapultepec, just outside Mexico City, started on September 13, 1847. One of the first American war correspondents, George Wilkins Kendall of the *New Orleans Daily Picayune*, filed this dispatch the following day:

City of Mexico, September 14, 1847—Another victory, glorious in its results and which has thrown luster upon the American arms, has been achieved today by the army under General Scott—the proud capital of Mexico has fallen into the power of a mere handful of men compared with the immense odds arrayed against them, and Santa Anna, instead of shedding his blood as he had promised, is wandering with the remnant of his army no one knows whither.

The apparently impregnable works on Chapultepec, after a desperate struggle, were triumphantly carried; Generals Bravo and Mouterde, besides a host of officers of different grades, taken prisoners; over one thousand non-commissioned officers and privates, all their cannon and ammunition, are in our hands; the fugitives were soon in full flight towards the different works which command the entrances to the city, and our men at once were in hot pursuit. . . .

At seven o'clock this morning, General Scott, with his staff, rode in and took quarters in the national palace, on the top of which the Stars and Stripes was already flying. An immense crowd of blanketed leperos, the scum of the capital, were congregated in the plaza as the commander-in-chief entered it. They pressed upon our soldiers and eyed them as though they were beings of another world. So much were they in the way, and with such eagerness did they press around, that General Scott was compelled to order our dragoons to clear the plaza. They were told, however, not to injure or harm a man in the crowd—they were all our friends!

Once more the power of Santa Anna was ended, and he resigned as president. The military victory brought an end, too, to the fighting. What remained was to negotiate the peace. Before the victory at Chapultepec, Trist had met with Mexican commissioners to talk about peace terms. At that time the Mexicans were unwilling to yield the land between the Nueces and the Rio Grande; they suggested a line from the Nueces to Santa Fe and then west to Monterey, California. Although Trist's instructions were to insist on the Rio Grande line, he submitted the Mexican proposal to Washington. Polk then recalled Trist. Secretary of State James Buchanan ordered him home but in a personal note wrote that if Trist had a peace treaty already written when the notice arrived, why, then, he might bring it back with him.

Trist later gave these reasons for disobeying the presidential order: The government still desired peace; time was important; Mexico was not going to surrender any more territory than his original instructions called for; and, amazingly, the president had ordered his recall through a lack of awareness of the situation. When Polk learned of Trist's refusal to return home, he termed the action "arrogant, impudent and very insulting to his government," but he said he would not automatically reject a treaty submitted by Trist.

In November, Mexico selected new peace commissioners,

and Trist concluded his negotiations with them at the village of Guadalupe Hidalgo, just north of Mexico City. The Mexicans, fearful that the Americans might want more, yielded to the three chief demands of the United States. They accepted the Rio Grande boundary, they ceded California and New Mexico to the United States, and they accepted as compensation $15 million instead of the $30 million they had been asking. In return, Trist agreed to assume the American monetary claims that were one of the causes of the war.

The treaty arrived in Washington on February 20, 1848, and the next day Polk summoned his cabinet. He told them he would submit the treaty to the Senate and gave these reasons:

> That the treaty conformed on the main question of limits and boundaries to the instructions given to Mr. Trist in April last; and that though, if the treaty were now to be made, I should demand more territory . . . yet it was doubtful whether this could ever be obtained by the consent of Mexico.
>
> . . . if I were now to reject a treaty made upon my own terms, as authorized in April last, with the unanimous approbation of the cabinet, the probability is that Congress would not grant either men or money to prosecute the war. Should this be the result, the army now in Mexico would be constantly wasting and diminishing in numbers, and I might at last be compelled to withdraw them, and thus lose the two provinces of New Mexico and Upper California, which were ceded to the United States by this treaty.

So the treaty was sent to the Senate, which on March 10 ratified it by a vote of thirty-eight to fourteen. On May 25 Mexico ratified the treaty too and peace once more descended upon the two countries. The boundary question was settled, in Article V of the treaty, as follows:

The boundary line between the two Republics shall commence in the Gulf of Mexico, three leagues from land, opposite the mouth of the Rio Grande, otherwise called the Rio Bravo del Norte, or opposite the mouth of its deepest branch, if it shall have more than one branch emptying directly into the sea; from thence up the middle of that river, following the deepest channel, where it has more than one, to the point where it strikes the southern boundary of New Mexico; thence, westwardly along the whole southern boundary of New Mexico (which runs north of the town called Paso) to its western termination; thence northward, along the western line of New Mexico, until it intersects the first branch of the river Gila (or if it should not intersect any branch of that river, then to the point on the said line nearest to such branch, and thence in a direct line to the same); thence down the middle of the said branch of the said river, until it empties into the Rio Colorado; thence across the Rio Colorado, following the division line between Upper and Lower California, to the Pacific Ocean.

The treaty further defined the southern and western limits of New Mexico as those laid down in the official United States map of Mexico drawn by J. Disturnell and published in New York in 1847.

The boundary line, then, was settled. The United States extended from sea to sea. It had grown by 530,706 square miles; added to the country was the area that would one day become the states of California and New Mexico and parts of Arizona, Utah, Colorado, and Nevada.

There were some unhappy consequences too. Polk, a strong party man and a vengeful politician, dismissed Trist from the State Department and did his best to humiliate Scott by relieving him of his command and calling him home to testify in a court of inquiry.

Of the four men in the field who had made the expansion

of the United States possible, three were victims of political vendettas: Kearny, Trist, and Scott. Only Taylor escaped; he was elected president, succeeding Polk in 1848.

Polk himself did not escape criticism. His political opponents called him "Polk the mendacious," but history has been kinder to him. Now he is generally regarded as one of the strong presidents of the United States, the man who brought more territory into the country than any other president with the exception of Thomas Jefferson.

|| 10 ||

The Gadsden Purchase

ANTONIO LÓPEZ DE SANTA ANNA became president of Mexico for the fourth time in 1853. A revolt, backed by the clergy and the large landowners, overthrew the government to forestall reforms set in motion by the revolutions of 1848 in Europe. Called back from exile to maintain order and to stifle the growing republican movement, Santa Anna responded eagerly. A new election was called, and on March 17, 1853, Santa Anna, a military hero to most Mexicans despite his defeats in Texas and in the Mexican-American War, was elected by an overwhelming majority.

The man who had exercised dictatorial power on three previous occasions as president (1833 to 1836; 1841 to 1844; and 1846 to 1847) immediately showed that he had not changed. He exiled his major political enemies; he abolished freedom of the press; he assumed all executive and legislative powers; he proclaimed himself "Serenissimo Altessa" (Serene Highness).

Within the first few months of the new regime in Mexico, its relations with the United States were strained again. Three different provisions of the Treaty of Guadalupe Hidalgo were involved.

First, the United States had promised to protect Mexico from Indians, mainly Apache, who lived in the United States and crossed the border to raid Mexico; but the United States had been unable to do so.

Second, the treaty provided for the use of Mexican soil for the construction of a transcontinental railroad along the Gila River, and there were strong pressures in the United States to seize or buy the land that was needed.

Third, a team of American and Mexican commissioners and surveyors was unable to agree on one key point on the border; the dispute involved six thousand square miles of land. This last was the most serious difference between the two countries, and it led directly to the Gadsden Purchase. It also led to the fourth and final overthrow of Santa Anna.

The peace treaty provided that the southeastern boundary line between the two countries was to begin in the Gulf of Mexico opposite the mouth of the Rio Grande, then up the middle of that river to "a point where it strikes the southern boundary of New Mexico (which runs north of the town called Paso) to its western termination." The New Mexican lines were defined as those shown on Disturnell's Map of the United States. The problem arose when the commissioners discovered that the map was in error. The town of El Paso del Norte (now Ciudad Juárez, Mexico) was not on the parallel of latitude 32°15′ N, as shown, but at 31°45′. The question was whether the southern boundary between the two nations should be located according to accurate degrees of latitude and longitude or eight miles above Paso as shown on the map.

The area involved, the Mesilla Valley, was arid and unproductive land, occupied by about three thousand persons, certainly not worth an international incident. Its importance to

Mexico was a matter of pride; most Mexicans thought the United States was a greedy land-grabber. Its importance to the United States had to do with passage of a transcontinental railroad, which would have to go through the valley because of the rugged mountains to the north.

When Franklin Pierce took the oath as president of the United States on March 4, 1853, he, like Polk, faced a serious dispute with his neighbor to the south. The American governor of New Mexico had taken formal possession of the Mesilla area. And the Mexican governor of Chihuahua had declared that he would preserve the national honor against all aggression. The Mexicans sent troops a thousand strong to the border, but both sides held off firing. Unlike Polk, Pierce decided to avoid war and negotiate a new treaty. He chose James Gadsden of South Carolina as ambassador to Mexico, with orders to settle the problem.

Gadsden was a strong Andrew Jackson man. He had served under Jackson in the Florida campaigns of 1817 and 1818; a fort in Florida was named for him; he had vigorously supported Jackson for the presidency in 1824. Since then he had served as a commissioner dealing with the Indians in Florida and had run unsuccessfully for several political offices in Florida. On returning to Charleston, South Carolina, he had become president of the Louisville, Cincinnati and Charleston Railroad. During the Mexican War he had opposed any large acquisition of Mexican land, but he believed that the United States should attempt to obtain a "natural boundary" based on mountains or rivers or deserts.

In his instructions Gadsden was urged to emphasize the friendly feelings of the United States toward Mexico, to state that neither country should take possession of the Mesilla Valley until the boundary was adjusted, to press for a change in the boundary line to put the proposed railroad route within the United States, and to settle all claims between the two nations. To accomplish all this, he was authorized to pay a "liberal sum."

Gadsden arrived in Mexico in August 1853 and immediately met with Santa Anna and his foreign minister. The Mexicans emphasized the failure of the Americans to control the Indians and to pay for the damages they had inflicted on Mexicans. It soon became quite clear that Mexico was greatly in need of money. Gadsden wrote to the secretary of state in Washington: "This is a government of plunder and necessity; we can rely on no other influence but an appeal to both."

By October, Washington had become convinced that another Mexican revolution was in the making and that the government might well be overturned. This could mean a delay in negotiating a favorable treaty, possibly a long delay.

A special messenger was sent to Mexico City bearing secret instructions to Gadsden about several possible boundary lines. The United States was willing to pay $50 million for northern lands in three Mexican states, Coahuila, Chihuahua, and Sonora, and for all of Lower California. The smallest of the areas sought was intended for the railroad line. For this area, along with a release of all claims under the Treaty of Guadalupe Hidalgo and the abrogation of the Indian clause, Gadsden was authorized to pay up to $15 million. He was instructed also to try to get a port on the Gulf of California for the United States.

The Mexicans, certain that the United States had military plans, were further alarmed when in November an American adventurer named William Walker, with fifty men, invaded Lower California and declared it an independent republic. Walker was dislodged, but the Mexicans, including Santa

Anna, were convinced that the Americans would take whatever land they wanted. He turned to Europe for aid, but no
country there would intervene.

Santa Anna was in serious political difficulties at home. A
revolution threatened, and unless he could equip an army, he
certainly would be overthrown. He also knew that if he went
to war with the United States, he would be deposed. It made
sense to avoid war by selling land to the United States and to
use the money to maintain himself in office. Despite the pressures on him, Santa Anna was patriotic enough to sell only
what was necessary. He told Gadsden that he would consider
yielding only enough land to give the United States the railroad route. His aides flatly refused to talk about selling Lower
California or any other land.

The negotiations went surprisingly quickly and were completed on December 30. The treaty, as signed that day, provided first for abrogation of the Indian clause but with the
proviso that the United States would help Mexico with the
Indian problem; second, for payment of $15 million to Mexico
and the assumption by the United States of American claims
against Mexico; third, there was a promise of mutual aid to
suppress filibustering expeditions against Mexico; and finally,
the following boundary line was set:

> Beginning in the Gulf of Mexico, three leagues from land,
> opposite the mouth of the Rio Grande, as provided in the
> fifth article of the treaty of Guadalupe Hidalgo; thence as
> defined in the said article, up the middle of that river to the
> point where the parallel of thirty-one degrees, forty-seven min-
> utes north latitude crosses the same; thence due west one
> hundred miles; thence south to the parallel of thirty-one de-
> grees, twenty minutes north latitude; thence along said parallel
> to the one hundred and eleventh meridian of longitude west of
> Greenwich; thence in a straight line to a point on the Colorado

River twenty English miles below the junction of the Gila and Colorado Rivers; thence up the middle of said river Colorado until it intersects the present line between the United States and Mexico.

Gadsden had seemingly achieved his objectives: the Mesilla Valley controversy was settled by the new boundary; the United States had its southern rail route to the Pacific; and the vexing Indian clause had been canceled. But when President Pierce sent the treaty to the Senate on February 10, 1854, he recommended some minor changes in it.

Several Northern senators saw in the Gadsden Treaty the acquisition of more slave lands and therefore opposed it. Some Californians opposed it because it did not include Lower California. Others regretted the failure to acquire a port on the Gulf of California. And still others bitterly opposed any payments to Santa Anna, whom they regarded as a tyrant. After voting on a series of amendments, the Senate took up the treaty itself on April 17. It was defeated by a vote of twenty-eight to eighteen, short of the necessary two-thirds.

The next day the Senate, led by Southern senators, adopted a resolution to reconsider the treaty. The amount of compensation to Mexico was fixed at $10 million ($5 million less than Gadsden had agreed to). The Indian abrogation clause was changed to eliminate a promise of future help to Mexico on the Indian problem. There was no mention of private claims (although Gadsden had agreed to accept responsibility for these claims). Finally, the amount of land to be acquired was reduced slightly, by nine thousand square miles, after the Senate voted on six different boundary lines. On April 25 the treaty was ratified by a vote of thirty-three to twelve. President Pierce reluctantly agreed to the revised treaty.

Gadsden then returned to Mexico. He was distressed by the alterations in the treaty and hoped that Santa Anna would reject it. But Santa Anna needed money desperately; the Mexicans signed. On June 21 President Pierce asked the House of Representatives to appropriate the money to pay for the land. Another debate about the treaty arose, in which conflicting railroad interests, slavery, the powers of the House of Representatives, and lack of information were all cited. The final vote was one hundred and five in favor, sixty-three opposed. On June 30, 1854, the Gadsden Treaty was adopted and Pierce proclaimed the land to be part of the United States.

Unfortunately, the treaty did not help United States–Mexican relations very much. The Mexican people persisted in their hatred for the United States and what they considered its illegal expansion. Santa Anna continued his hostility toward the United States, although he accepted its money. Gadsden at one point suspended diplomatic relations between himself, as ambassador, and the Mexican government. Three times Mexico demanded that the United States recall Gadsden, whose distaste for Santa Anna was not well disguised, but the demands were refused.

A revolution in Mexico finally caught up with Santa Anna, however, and he was forced to abdicate on August 8, 1855. Gadsden welcomed the liberals who took over the Mexican government, but the hostility of American speculators to Gadsden increased because he refused to help them. On March 10, 1856, four companies of United States dragoons took formal possession of the new territory in Tucson. Three months later Gadsden was recalled from his post as ambassador to Mexico, a victim of behind-the-scenes pressure by land and railroad speculators in Washington.

Thus the fairly level route between El Paso and San Diego, a wagon route that had first been traversed by Lieutenant Colonel Philip St. George Cooke in 1847 in support of General

Kearny's conquest of New Mexico and California, passed into American hands.

In 1857 the first stagecoaches rolled across the area—largely desert—and in the following year the Butterfield Overland Mail started regular service west of El Paso. The stagecoach route was the fastest between East and West until the railroads were finally built. In 1879 and 1880 the Southern Pacific Railroad track between El Paso and Yuma was completed and the promise of the Gadsden Purchase was realized.

Alaska

CAPTAIN VITUS JONASSEN BERING, an officer in the Imperial Russian Navy, had important news for the czar. He had just completed a voyage of exploration in the oceans east of Siberia, and now he knew the answers to some of the puzzling geographic questions that had been asked for years. He had landed on the Kamchatka Peninsula, thousands of miles from St. Petersburg, and had no way to communicate with his superiors. It was September 1728. In front of Bering lay the fog-covered Sea of Okhotsk and, beyond, the vast wilderness of Siberia with its endless steppes, marshes, forests, and snow-capped mountains.

Bering was a Dane who had been serving in the Russian navy for twenty-five years. Three years earlier he had come across trackless frozen areas, bringing with him materials and supplies to build ships for his explorations of the frigid oceans to the east. His ocean trip was now completed; ahead of him lay the equally dangerous crossing of Siberia. There was only one way to return. He and a party of his men packed their provisions on supply animals, mounted their horses, and started off westward. Plodding step by step, day after day, week after week, month after month, it took Bering a year and a half to complete the land journey. He arrived in St. Petersburg on March 1, 1730.

This was the story he told to the members of the Admiralty College: On July 14, 1728, he and his crew sailed north from the Kamchatka Peninsula on a ship they had built there, the *Saint Gabriel*. The voyage was comparatively easy; the wind was fair and they encountered no storms or fog. On August 8 they discovered a large island, which they named St. Lawrence Island. (This later became part of Alaska.) Pushing farther north, they rounded East Cape, the easternmost point of Siberia, on August 15 and found that the coastline turned westward. There was no land visible to the north; they saw nothing but fog to the east.

Bering had sailed through the strait that now bears his name. He had proved to his own satisfaction that the continent of Asia was separated by an ocean from America to the east. Although on a clear day in Bering Strait both Asia and America can be seen, on that day in 1728 Bering did not see any part of North America. Afraid to proceed because of the oncoming winter, Bering returned to Kamchatka.

Instead of receiving a hero's welcome in St. Petersburg, Bering was questioned sharply about his findings. There was no proof of what lay to the east, some said. Had he really demonstrated that Asia and America were separated? It was a disappointing reception for Bering.

The Admiralty College finally decided that only another expedition could prove the point. In typically bureaucratic fashion, it was almost three years before orders were completed for the expedition. Bering left St. Petersburg in 1733, and this time it took him nearly four years to traverse Siberia with his men, materials, and supplies—everything except wood had to be taken with them. Some of it got lost. Some of his men died en route.

In 1737 Bering arrived at Okhotsk. His first job was to build barracks, storehouses, and warehouses. When these were finished, he started construction of two ships, each eighty feet long and twenty feet wide, and drawing about nine feet of water. Named the *Saint Paul* and the *Saint Peter*, they were launched in 1740. Bering and his men sailed around the long tip of Kamchatka and arrived at Avatcha Bay on the east coast of the peninsula in the fall, to spend the winter there. He gave the name of Petropavlosk to his base on Avatcha Bay.

In May 1741 Bering met with his aides to discuss the coming voyage. He commanded the *Saint Peter*, with a crew of seventy-seven, including a German-born naturalist, Georg Wilhelm Steller. Alexei Chirikov commanded the *Saint Paul*, with seventy-five men aboard. The officers were certain that the unknown shores of America lay due east or northeast, but the map they had, which had been made in St. Petersburg, showed that land was to the southeast. They decided to follow the map and their instructions first and, if land were not found to the southeast, to turn north and east.

A month later, on June 4, 1741, with a light southerly wind behind them, the two vessels sailed from Avatcha Bay. They made their way south, following the charts for a week before turning north. Because of changing winds, fog, and rain, the two vessels lost sight of each other. From then on, the ships made their way separately, each one trying to fulfill the purposes of the expedition.

On June 23 Chirikov on the *Saint Paul* turned east and by July 11 spotted driftwood and gulls, a sure sign of land. At two o'clock on the morning of July 15, at a latitude of 55°21′, Chirikov's crew saw high, wooded mountains ahead. As day broke, the coast of America (near Cape Addington) was visible three miles off.

A boat was lowered, but it could not find a landing spot. A wind arose during the evening, and the ship made its way slowly north. Sometimes fog hid the coastline. It was not until two days later, on July 17, that the Russians found an entrance to a large bay at 57°15′ and sent a boat ashore.

Alexei Chirikov, a man unknown to Americans, had "discovered" America from the Pacific.

For several days his landing party was not heard from. Chirikov then sent another boat, his only remaining small one, to look for the missing men. But it too disappeared. The Russians obviously were on a hostile shore. The next day two small canoes manned by Indians approached but were frightened away. The Russians came to the conclusion that their shipmates had been captured and murdered.

While Chirikov pondered his next step, a strong west wind arose, and he was forced to put out to sea. A meeting of officers decided that further attempts to explore the land were not feasible. With their small boats gone, there was no chance to refill their water casks. They sailed west and saw land once more, probably the island of Unalaska in the Aleutian chain. As they continued on, their water dwindled and rations were cut. Scurvy broke out, the crew grew weaker, some died. In October, however, land appeared on the horizon, and Chirikov arrived at Avatcha. Twenty-one men had died on the voyage, but Chirikov was home.

Meanwhile Bering too had changed course. On July 15, the same day that Chirikov saw land, Bering's crew saw sea otters in the water and Steller thought he saw land. But it was not until the next day, July 16, that a lookout reported towering peaks on the land. The log of the *Saint Peter* recorded the event:

At 12:30 we sighted high snow-covered mountains and among
them a high volcano, N by W.

Their landfall was Mount St. Elias, eighteen thousand feet
high. For a few days they cruised along the shore, looking at
the beautiful forests and level beaches. On July 20 they went
ashore to fill their water casks at Kayak Island.

Steller, the German naturalist, was quite excited. He found
remains of fire and scattered bones, shell heaps and dried fish,
smoked salmon, and bows and arrows. He gathered samples
and wanted to stay longer to continue his studies. Bering,
believing that his mission was accomplished, was adamant. If
Steller did not come back to the ship, it would sail without
him. Despite Steller's protests, Bering insisted. Steller had
only ten hours ashore for his scientific observations. In his
diary he wrote:

> The American continent (on this side) as far as climate is con-
> cerned, is notably better than the extreme northeastern part
> of Asia. For although the land, however it faces the sea, whether
> we looked at it from far or near, consists of amazingly high
> mountains, most of which had the peaks covered with perpetual
> snow, yet these mountains, in comparison with those of Asia,
> are of a better nature and character.

Bering, now sixty-one and less than enthusiastic about new
discoveries, did not even leave the ship. He had seen America
and he wanted to return home as quickly as possible. An
experienced captain in the treacherous waters of the north,
he was worried about the return trip. He wrote in his note-
book:

> We think we have discovered everything, but we do not stop
> to think where we are, how far we are still from home and what
> may happen. Who knows but perhaps contrary winds will come

up and prevent us from returning. We do not know this country
nor do we have any provisions for wintering here.

Before long, Bering's forebodings were confirmed. A fair
wind came up on July 21, and Bering ordered his ship to sail,
without even waiting for all the water casks to be ready. But
then the winds changed; they made little progress in the fog
and mist, their water started to run out, and scurvy, the dread
disease of seafaring, broke out among the crew. In mid-
August they were still hundreds of miles from Kamchatka. On
August 30 they anchored near an island they called Shumagin,
after a sailor who died of scurvy there. Bering himself fell ill.

From then on, the terrors of the sea mounted. A violent
storm that lasted seventeen days drove the ship southward.
Scurvy spread among the crew and a man died almost every
day. Despite their illness, the sailors worked day and night,
in the cold, rain, snow, and fog. By late October only fifteen
casks of drinking water remained. On November 4, when only
ten men in the entire crew could even move, land was sighted.
The anchors of the *Saint Peter* went down offshore, but a huge
wave lifted the ship over a rock ledge and carried it into
smoother water. It was clear to all that they would have to
stay for the winter.

The sick men were carried ashore. It was a desolate island,
with no game or birds in sight for food. Sea otters were killed
and eaten, their skins cured. The survivors came across the
rotting carcass of a whale on the beach and ate it. Steller
searched for antiscurvy herbs and plants in the snow-crusted
earth. The men used whale blubber to make lanterns. Their
major problem was survival, and their chief enemy was the
bold, ferocious Arctic blue fox, which showed no fear of men.
The foxes attacked the living and ate the dead. Gloom and
despair fell over the survivors as winter came in its full fury.

On December 8, 1741, Bering died in a miserable hut scooped out of the sand banks near the shore and covered over with a few logs. By January only the toughest of the men had survived. They made expeditions to find food, and even if there was only a rotting whale, they forced themselves to eat it. Then spring came, and so did the sea cows.

Ancient mariners had sometimes mistaken these thirty-foot-long mammals for mermaids. Steller had the opportunity to examine live sea cows and dissect dead ones; he was the only naturalist in history to study live specimens, because by 1768 greedy fur hunters had exterminated the species. Most important to the crew, he discovered that the flesh of the sea cow was edible. The health of the survivors began to improve.

The men decided to build a new boat from the timbers of the *Saint Peter*. By August 1742 they had completed a thirty-six-foot-long boat, also named the *Saint Peter*, and on the thirteenth of August, forty-six men sailed from the island to which they had given Bering's name. After an uneventful voyage they arrived back at Avatcha Bay on August 27, carrying with them a cargo of sea-otter furs.

Thus ended Bering's voyage of exploration. It had been disastrous in terms of lives lost, but it had added considerably to the picture of the New World. Bering's assistant, Chirikov, was actually the first Russian to see the New World, but Bering is generally given the credit and his name has come down in history in many of the geographical features of the north: Bering Sea, Bering Strait, Bering Island.

The Russians discovered Alaska in 1741, two hundred years after the Spanish reached the Pacific Ocean much farther to the south. The Spanish were not interested in moving north from their missions in Mexico and California, but England had designs on the northernmost lands. Captain James Cook, aboard the *Resolution*, laid claim to parts of the coast in 1778 as he searched for a waterway between the Pacific and the Atlantic Oceans. He then sailed south to the Sandwich Islands (Hawaiian Islands). But the Russians had arrived first in Alaska.

Unlike the English and the French, the Russians were interested not in territory as such but in furs and the profits that went with them. The fur hunters of Siberia, the *promyshlenniki*, had ranged far and wide through the wintry wilderness, killing sable and other fur-bearing animals for sale to the Chinese. Now the sable was disappearing; the fur hunters were greedy and the supply of fur-bearing animals fell off. When the remnants of Bering's crew came to port with their sea-otter skins, some of which sold for three hundred rubles in gold in China, the Russian fur merchants began to organize to tap the sea-otter riches of America.

The Merchants Guild of Irkutsk, the center of the fur trade, tried to get the government to intervene to help them. But Catherine the Great said in 1769: "It is for traders to traffic where they please. I will furnish neither men nor ships nor money." A few years later, when a colonization project was under discussion, she remarked: "England's experience with American colonies should be a warning to other nations to abstain from such efforts."

A fur trader and self-made capitalist, Grigory Shelekhov decided that he would organize a permanent colony in Alaska anyway and obtain control of the lucrative fur trade. In 1783 he built three ships and sailed from Okhotsk with 192 men and a cargo of cattle and seeds. He landed on Kodiak Island, just southeast of the Aleutians, and built a settlement there. After four years, however, the number of furs being sent off was not considerable and it became apparent that his idea, although good, called for more men in the field and a more efficient organization. He returned to Irkutsk but failed in his attempts to obtain a monopoly of the trade. He saw the need for an ambitious, able, and more active manager for the Alaska enterprise, and he found the man he wanted.

Aleksandr Andreyevich Baranov, born in 1746, emigrated to Siberia in 1780 and managed a glass factory there. He went into the fur-trading business, selling guns, powder, and shot to the natives in exchange for otter skins, but on his first big venture he found that the natives used the guns to take the skins back from him. With no resources but his own ability and his ambition to rise in the class-conscious society of Russia, Baranov listened to Shelekhov and accepted his offer to manage the Kodiak Island outpost. On July 8, 1791, he landed in Kodiak. He found five or six cabins, a bunkhouse, a blacksmith shop, and a fur storehouse. More important, he discovered that the supply of furs on Kodiak was about exhausted; he would have to find a new source of furs if he was to succeed.

There was only one direction to go—to the coast of Alaska. Everywhere there were rivals. English, French, and American ships sailed freely up and down the coast, buying a rich harvest of sea-otter skins. They paid (in trading goods) higher prices than the Russians; they had no permanent settlements to maintain; they were better sailors and navigators than the Russians.

Baranov got down to work in 1792 and reinforced a small settlement on Cook's Inlet (near Kenai Peninsula and Prince William Sound). In two years he completed the first ship built in the north, the *Phoenix*, seventy-three feet long. She sailed for Kodiak on September 4 and in the spring of 1795 arrived at Okhotsk. In 1796 Baranov founded a colony on Yakutat Island near Mount St. Elias, the area where Bering had first seen America. Despite hostile Indians, awful weather, and competition from the English and the Americans, his colonies prospered.

Shelekhov had died in 1795 in Russia, and his interests had been taken over by his son-in-law, Nikolay Rezanov. Catherine the Great had died, too, and had been succeeded by Paul I. Rezanov became a companion of the new czar, and before long the fur merchants of Irkutsk, who had organized a United American Company, were granted a monopoly by the czar. The new company was called the Russian American Company; it had full privileges for twenty years on the coast of northwestern America, with exclusive right to all enterprises, whether hunting, trading, or building.

In America, Baranov saw that the only way to forestall British and American pressure was to move south, to establish a colony and a base for trading, thus keeping the competition out. He selected as his site Sitka Island (now called Baranof Island, where the city of Sitka is located). In 1799 an armada of 550 canoes, with a hundred Russians and their wives aboard, and almost nine hundred friendly Aleut Indians, attempted to land. A squall came up, drenching them and overturning their boats. And the Indians on the land fired at them. Almost a hundred of the Russian party lost their lives, and Baranov returned to his base at Yakutat, near Mount St. Elias.

He tried again on July 28. This time he returned to Sitka with a peaceful approach. Twenty Kolosh Indians came out of the woods. Their chief was Ska-out-lelt, an impressive-looking man six feet tall, with coarse black hair tied in a knot on the back of his head. The Russians offered to pay for the site with guns, clothes, copper, and iron. The Indians accepted. The Russians came ashore and started to build a settlement they called Fort St. Michael. It was almost completed in the spring of 1800, when Yankee traders arrived. Baranov was shocked to find that they were paying four pounds of lead and powder for an otter skin, much more than the Russians offered.

A view of Sitka in a watercolor done around 1860. The governor's mansion is the large building on the right. The Indian settlement on the left is separated from the rest of the city by a stockade. *Alaska State Museum, Juneau.*

Still Baranov managed to send off fur shipments, but troubles mounted in the new colonies. Baranov had not heard from Russia in four years when finally in 1802 a courier arrived at his headquarters in Kodiak with the good news about the organization of the new company, in which he was granted some stock. He was also given the Cross of Saint Vladimir "for faithful service" and appointed governor of the colonies. The courier also reported that Paul I had died and that Alexander was the new czar.

At Sitka the Indians, who had never been content with the presence of the Russians, decided to wipe them out. On June 20 Ska-out-lelt led his warriors in a surprise attack and killed most of the Russian settlers, torturing prisoners and setting fire to the fort. Only a handful survived. In the spring of 1803 Baranov, now fifty-six, became obsessed with the idea of reconquering Sitka. He strengthened his base at Yakutat, made a fast canoe trip to Sitka to reconnoiter the land, and decided to attack as soon as possible.

In the midst of his preparations, at Yakutat, on April 4, 1804, a canoe came in from Unalaska with a letter for Baranov. It read: "We do confer upon the said Aleksandr Andreyevich the rank in Civil Service of Collegiate Councilor." It was signed by the czar himself.

The letter marked the achievement of Baranov's lifelong ambition. A man without formal education, who had never even been accepted by the merchants' guild in Russia, was now a nobleman, entitled to be called "Excellency." His rank was equivalent to that of a colonel in the army or an abbot in the church. Baranov wrote a letter of humble thanks to the czar and another, not quite so humble, to the directors of the Russian American Company. He said:

> I am now a nobleman, but Sitka is destroyed. I cannot live under the burden, so I am going forth either to restore the possession of my august benefactor or to die in the attempt.

It took a long time to prepare the expedition against Sitka. In September 1804 Baranov called his four hundred men together on the sandy beach at Yakutat to pray for success. With a few ships and dozens of canoes, he set out for Sitka Sound, and, on arrival, he found a pleasant surprise. A Russian frigate, the *Neva*, a large, powerful ship, was there. At Hawaii the captain had heard about the destruction at Sitka and had received orders to go north and help Baranov.

Baranov at first tried to negotiate with the silent, unfriendly Indians who met them. He demanded that the Aleut captives be returned and that all Kolosh Indians leave the island.

Impossible, replied Chief Kot-le-an, nephew of Ska-out-lelt.

He explained that the island had been the home of the Sitka Indians since their beginning, and held their totems and spirits.

Baranov was adamant. He delivered an ultimatum: Evacuate the fort and get off the island or he would blow them all into the sea.

Kot-le-an agreed to deliver the captives and let the Russians build a new fort, but not to leave. Baranov insisted. Kot-le-an left the conference quietly. Impatient, Baranov decided to attack.

He did so on October 1, but the Indians repulsed the Russians, wounding Baranov on the arm. For two days the Indians tried to compromise, offering to leave hostages as a guarantee of good conduct, but Baranov was not moved. During the night the Russians heard a strange wailing song that ended only an hour before dawn. In the morning the Russians found a horrible sight. The Kolosh had killed many of their own children and had fled from their ancestral home.

In New Archangel (near Sitka) the Russians spent a miserable winter. The Indians stayed on in the outlying areas, shooting any Russian they could. The food was meager in the encampment; there was scurvy, but the men managed to survive until spring, when ships and traders arrived again. With the good weather, the Russians built better shelter for themselves and a fort for protection.

In August 1805 Nikolay Rezanov, a key figure in the operation of the company in Russia, arrived. Critical at first because he had not understood the operation in the field, he now saw the working reality. He stayed the winter and wrote to the other directors of the company that Baranov was "an extraordinary person." He added:

His name is famed the length of the Pacific. The Bostonians esteem and respect him, and savage tribes, in dread of him, offer him friendship from the most distant places.

The winter was bad as usual. Sixty of the nearly two hundred Russians there suffered from scurvy. And the camp faced a constant threat of annihilation by the Indians, who respected the power of Baranov but resented the invasion of their lands. As a first step, the Indians carefully planned an attack on the settlement at Yakutat Island. They succeeded in killing all but a few of the settlers and in destroying the buildings. Thousands of Indians then converged on Sitka, which appeared to be helpless. Only the timely appearance of an American ship, with cannons primed for action, saved the colony.

Baranov was a curious mixture of optimism and pessimism. Far from cowed by the Indian menace, he talked of expansion, to the Columbia River, to California, to the Hawaiian Islands. At other times he was depressed; he wanted to be relieved of his responsibilities. He convinced Rezanov, who was returning to St. Petersburg after a trip to California, to find a replacement for him. But Rezanov fell from a horse while crossing Siberia and died of his injuries.

In New Archangel the situation began to improve. Baranov built a governor's residence, which was called "Baranov's Castle," and also houses for a thousand settlers. Military discipline was imposed on the colony—and it thrived.

The years of privation seemed to be over. Baranov lived like a monarch. He wore black silk waistcoats, slippers with silver buckles. On his lapels were the Cross of Saint Vladimir and the Order of Saint Anne of the Second Class. He had a library of more than a thousand books. At his table he welcomed visitors from all over. They feasted on wild duck, venison, salmon; and they drank well too. Everything seemed to be going well.

One day, however, Baranov found some charred papers in a stove. The papers charged him with inhuman feeling, arbitrary exercise of power. The plotters drew up a declaration of independence, prepared to set up a republic, and talked of condemning him to death. Baranov was stunned. The plot was thwarted, but Baranov was a changed man. He spent the winter alone, drinking and worrying; he despaired of the future.

By the spring of 1810 Baranov bounced back. He learned that a replacement for him had been chosen and was on his way. And he prepared an expedition, which left in 1811, to establish a settlement in California, at Fort Ross, ninety miles north of San Francisco, the farthest south Russia had penetrated in North America.

Two years later bad news again reached Baranov. The ship carrying the new commander for Sitka had been lost; his replacement had died at sea. Convinced that it was the will of God for him never to return home, Baranov concentrated more than ever on the affairs of the settlement. He bought ships, expanded trade, sent more furs back to Russia.

In 1818 Baranov, now seventy-two, turned the keys of his establishment over to his replacements, two naval officers of the czar. He spent seven months unraveling his accounts (and refuted the critics who had so sharply criticized his operations). He had established twenty-four settlements in North America, built eight ships, built up the financial worth of the Russian American Company to more than seven million rubles (more than $5 million), and provided the stockholders with profits of as much as ninety percent of their investments. His accounts finished, Baranov decided to return to Russia. Before he left, his old Indian opponent Kot-le-an came to see him.

"We have hated you," he said. "Fourteen years we have planned revenge."

Silence.

"Now we are old men together and are about to die. Let us be brothers."

Baranov agreed.

He sailed from Alaska on December 1. While at sea, on April 13, 1819, he died. The Russian occupation of Alaska, which had resulted in growth and great profits, started deteriorating. The charter of the Russian American Company was renewed twice more, but control of the company passed from the independent merchants to the government and profits began to decline.

The momentum for expansion died down. In 1841 the Russians sold Fort Ross, their outpost in California, to John A. Sutter, the Swiss emigrant who founded Sutter Fort (near Sacramento). The stock value of the company declined; it started to lose money. The third charter expired on December 31, 1861, and was not renewed. It was clear to all that Alaska was now a liability to the Russians.

Even before this, there had been talk that the Russians might sell Alaska. During the Crimean War, in 1854, when the Russians and the British were fighting, the sale of Alaska to prevent its capture by the British was mentioned. In 1856 some Americans proposed buying it, and in 1860 President James Buchanan considered negotiations with Russia. But the project did not really get under way until the end of the Civil War in the United States—and the initiative came from the Russians.

Late in 1866 the Russians decided to sell Alaska to the United States. They had several reasons: the financial decline of the Russian American Company; its inability to defend itself; lack of interest in governing it; and friendship for the

United States. The Russian minister Edouard Stoeckl raised the question with Secretary of State William H. Seward on March 9, 1867, and within three weeks an agreement was reached. The United States would pay $7,200,000, and it would gain possession of Alaska. The treaty gave these geographical limits to Alaska:

Commencing from the southernmost point of the island called Prince of Wales Island, which point lies in the parallel of fifty-four degrees, forty minutes north latitude, and between the one hundred and thirty-first and one hundred and thirty-third degree of west longitude (meridian of Greenwich), the said line shall ascend to the north along the channel called Portland channel, as far as the point of the continent where it strikes the fifty-sixth degree of north latitude; from this last mentioned point, the line of demarcation shall follow the summit of the mountains situated parallel to the coast as far as the point of intersection of the one hundred and forty-first degree of west longitude (of the same meridian); and finally, from said point of intersection, the said meridian line of the one hundred and forty-first degree, in its prolongation as far as the Frozen ocean. . . .

The western limit within which the territories and dominion conveyed are contained, passes through a point in Bering's straits on the parallel of sixty-five degrees thirty minutes north latitude, at its intersection by the meridian which passes midway between the islands of Krusenstern, or Ignalook, and the island of Ratmanoff, or Noonarbook, and proceeds due north, without limitation, into the same Frozen ocean. The same western limit, beginning at the same initial point, proceeds thence in a course nearly southwest, through Bering's straits and Bering's sea, so as to pass midway between the northwest point of the island of St. Lawrence and the southeast point of Cape Choukotski; to the meridian of one hundred and seventy-two degrees west longitude; thence from the intersection of that

Emmanuel Leutze's 1867 oil painting portrays some of the figures involved in the purchase of Alaska, including (*second from left*) Secretary of State Seward; (*standing, right foreground*) Russian minister Stoeckl; and (*second from right*) Senator Charles Summer. *Alaska State Museum, Juneau.*

meridian, in a southwesterly direction, so as to pass midway between the island of Attu and the Copper Island of the Kormandorski couplet or group in the North Pacific Ocean, to the meridian of one hundred and ninety-three degrees west longitude, so as to include in the territory conveyed the whole of the Aleutian Islands east of that meridian.

The treaty was signed at four o'clock in the morning on March 30, 1867, only eight hours before the adjournment of Congress. Seward tried to secure the ratification of the treaty before the members of Congress left town, but it appeared that the necessary two-thirds vote could not be obtained. The treaty was referred to the Senate Foreign Relations

Committee, but the vote was not taken until a special session of Congress was called in April.

The arguments for the purchase were basically economic, that Alaskan ports, mines, waters, furs, fisheries would be of untold value to the United States. The negative side was expressed by the *New York Tribune*, which said: "We simply obtain by the treaty the nominal possession of impassable deserts of snow, vast tracts of dwarf timbers, inaccessive mountain ranges, with a few islands where the climate is more moderate and a scanty population supported by fishing and trading with the Indians." The Senate barely ratified the treaty, twenty-seven votes for and twelve opposed.

The ceremonies that transferred Alaska to the United States took place on October 18, 1867, in Sitka. The United States commissioner, Brigadier General Lovell H. Rousseau, was accompanied by two hundred soldiers, sailors, and marines, who gathered around a ninety-foot flagpole. Russian officers were there too, but few Russian civilians; they were not happy about the transfer. Captain Alexei Pestchouroff, the Russian commissioner, ordered the double-eagle ensign of Russia to be lowered—ending 126 years of Russian rule. The Russian and American troops presented arms, and the ships in the harbor fired a twenty-one-gun salute.

Captain Pestchouroff turned to General Rousseau and said, "By the authority of his Majesty the Emperor of all Russias, I transfer to you, the agent of the United States, all the territory and dominion now possessed by his Majesty on the continent of America and in the adjacent islands, according to a treaty made between the two powers."

General Rousseau replied, "I accept from you, as agent of his Majesty the Emperor of all Russias, the territory and dominion which you have transferred to me, as commissioner on the part of the United States to receive the same."

His fifteen-year-old-son, George, assisted by a sailor, raised the United States flag to the top of the flagpole. Russian and American guns thundered another salute. Alaska was now part of the United States.

But it had not yet been paid for. Almost eight months of debate in Congress ensued before the money was appropriated. The debate raged all over the country too, and in it Alaska received many of the epithets that have come down to this day: Seward's Folly, Icebergia, Polaria, Walrussia. One newspaper said: "Russia has sold us a sucked orange." The *New York Herald* described Alaska as "an ice-house, a worthless desert." The opposition was more vocal than actual, and the appropriation was finally passed in July 1868.

For years Alaska was a neglected possession of the United States, governed by the military. Not until seventeen years after the purchase did Congress provide for the appointment of a civilian governor.

The discovery of gold in the Klondike in 1896 sparked a boom—and brought to a head a serious boundary dispute. The border between Russian Alaska and British Canada had been defined by a treaty in 1825 and adopted by the United States in 1867. There was no question about the northern part of the line, the 141st parallel. It was the southern section, between Portland Channel and Mount St. Elias, that caused the difficulty as the gold rushers flocked in. The treaties provided the following:

That whenever the summit of the mountains which extend in a direction parallel to the coast, from the fifty-sixth degree of north latitude to the point of intersection of the one hundred and forty-first degree of west longitude, shall prove to be at the distance of more than ten marine leagues [almost thirty-five miles] from the Ocean, the limit between the British possessions and the line of the coast which is to belong to Russia

Women prospectors on their way to the Klondike to search for gold. *Library of Congress.*

(and now to the United States) shall be formed by a line parallel to the windings of the coast, and which may never exceed the distance of ten marine leagues therefrom.

The British claimed that the line should follow the general outlines of the coast, some thirty miles inland, crossing the heads of many inlets that jutted into the continent. This would give them water access to British Columbia and the gold fields to the north. The Americans claimed that the line should follow the mountains or, if they were too far inland, the actual windings of the much indented coastline. A joint commission was set up in 1903 and it supported the American position.

In 1906 Congress empowered Alaska to elect a delegate to sit, without voting privileges, in Congress. The area became an organized territory in 1912 and in the following year elected a territorial legislature to sit in Juneau, the capital. Alaska made its first attempt to become a state in 1916, when a bill for statehood was introduced in Congress, but the sourdoughs (called that because of the lumps of dough they carried in their packs to bake bread while prospecting) preferred things as they were. Alaska became an important military base in World War II and, after the war, it waged a campaign for statehood in every session of Congress.

These efforts succeeded on June 30, 1958, when the Senate voted statehood. The *New York Times* the next morning carried an eight-column headline, its biggest, that said:

ALASKA TO JOIN UNION AS THE 49TH STATE:
FINAL APPROVAL IS VOTED BY SENATE, 64–20;
BILL SENT TO EISENHOWER, WHO WILL SIGN IT

From Anchorage, Alaska's largest city, Lawrence E. Davies of the *Times* reported:

Alaskans were stunned today by the realization that Congress had finally invited them to become "first class citizens."

Here in the territorial metropolis, the center of much of the agitation for statehood, it took them a while to get their bearings.

Long after the civil defense whistles had blown, signaling the Senate's action preparing the way for a forty-ninth star on the flag, unbelieving crowds almost silently walked the streets amid the tooting of automobile horns.

Stores did business as usual. A woman traffic policeman rode her motorcycle down Fourth Avenue putting tickets on cars that were parked overtime.

Some amateur photographers gleefully "shot" a passing car

bearing Texas license plates, emblematic of a state that would have to give up its much-loved stories of bigness as Alaska completes the transition to statehood.

Rita Martin, queen of the annual Fur Rendezvous, climbed a fire truck ladder and pinned a huge silver star—the forty-ninth—to a 60-by-40 flag hurriedly draped over the front wall of the Federal Building.

President Dwight D. Eisenhower signed the bill and Alaska formally became the forty-ninth state of the Union at two minutes past noon on January 3, 1959, ninety-two years after its purchase from Russia.

12

Hawaii

LATE IN JANUARY 1778 the natives of the Hawaiian island of Kauai looked south to sea and saw an astonishing sight. Two large floating islands with great white clouds on top were slowly approaching. A Hawaiian legend describes the reaction of the natives:

> One said to another: "What is that great thing with branches?" Others said: "It is a forest that has slid down into the sea," and the noise and the gabble was great. Others shouted: "It is a great double canoe for the sea monster of Mana."

What they saw in fact were two English ships, the *Discovery* and the *Resolution*, both commanded by Captain James Cook, the famous British explorer. It was their first sight of foreign sailing ships and of white men. The chief ordered some of his men to go in a canoe to examine the wonderful objects. Unafraid, they approached the British ships, and the legend recalls their first impressions of the white men: "men with white foreheads, shining eyes, wrinkled skins, square-cornered heads; the words of these men were indistinct and fire was in their mouths."

The Hawaiians were greatly impressed by these strange men who ate fire (smoked pipes) and took food from openings in their clothes (the Hawaiians had never before seen clothing with pockets). They were certain that these men were gods.

Captain Cook recorded his impressions:

> I tied some brass medals to a rope and gave them to those in one of the canoes, who, in return, tied some small mackerel to the rope, as an equivalent. This was repeated, and some small nails, or bits of iron, which they valued more than any other article, were given to them. For these, they exchanged some fish and a sweet potato, a sure sign that they had some notion of bartering, or, at least, of returning one present for another.

The Hawaiians were avid for anything made of iron, which was more valuable to them than jewels. For one nail they traded enough pork to feed a ship's company for a day. Cook also traded hatchets, knives, and trinkets for fish, fowl, coconuts, bananas, and other fruit. Life was fairly easy for the Hawaiians. The sea around them and the fertile soil of the islands produced more than enough for them. They received strangers easily; the women were attractive and the men friendly. Cook's crew, who had been at sea for almost two years, were overwhelmed by hospitality.

Captain Cook had sailed from England in July 1776, the month the Declaration of Independence was adopted in the United States, on his third and what proved to be his last voyage of exploration. The fifty-year-old captain had explored the ocean regions around the Society Islands, far to the south, and his mission now was to try to find a passage between the Atlantic and the Pacific from the Pacific side. He spent eight weeks on the island of Kauai, naming the group of islands the

Sandwich Islands, after his patron, the earl of Sandwich. He then sailed north to the coast of North America.

As winter approached, Cook sailed south once more to warm, hospitable Hawaii. He arrived at Maui first and then, on January 17, 1779, at Kealakekua Bay on the west coast of the island of Hawaii, largest of the islands. Word of his previous trip had spread through all the islands, and on his arrival he was accorded a welcome worthy of a god. Ten thousand people, in canoes, on surfboards, or just swimming, greeted him and his crew. One historian quotes the natives of the time: "The ancestral god has come back, for this is the time of the annual consecration."

Wherever Cook went ashore, people threw themselves on the ground as he passed, for it was not proper for mortals to gaze upon gods. Every day the Hawaiians sent pigs and vegetables to the ship. King Kalaniopuu visited Cook on the ship and presented him with feather cloaks, symbols of royalty. Cook gave the king a linen shirt, a sword, and a tool chest.

Despite a few misunderstandings, the visit ended harmoniously, and Cook sailed in February. Unluckily, a storm arose and damaged a mast on the *Resolution*, and Cook was forced to return to Kealakekua. This time, however, the harbor was silent. King Kalaniopuu had put the district under a religious taboo so that the people could relax from the taxing visit of the gods.

When Cook returned, the atmosphere was strained. One of the chiefs, who no longer believed that the white men were gods, stole one of the ship's small boats. Cook barred the natives from his ships. Two chiefs, ignorant of the ban, approached in a canoe and were fired upon. One was killed.

King Kalaniopuu, his royal feather cloak about his shoulders, was on the beach talking to Cook when he heard the news of the death of one of his chiefs. The king refused an

A portrait of Captain James Cook painted just before his last voyage.
National Maritime Museum, London.

invitation to follow Cook aboard the ship. Cook seized his hands to pull him forward. A chief struck Cook with a spear, and the Englishman groaned—whereupon the chief came to the conclusion that the white man was not a god, for a god would not cry out in pain.

The natives rushed to attack. Some of them fell before the fire of British marines. Cook waved to the small boats in the water to come into shore and pick him and his men up. As he did so, a club hit him on the head and he fell into the water. He struggled up, but he was hit again. He fell, mortally wounded. Thus ended Cook's last voyage of discovery.

He had discovered the Hawaiian Islands, at a vital crossroads in the Pacific Ocean, rather late in the era of great explorations. The islands are not far across the wide Pacific. They are two thousand miles from San Francisco; in geographic terms, just off the western coast of the United States. They include eight major inhabited islands, of which Cook saw about half, and a large number of smaller ones.

They lie in the Equatorial Zone, just below the Tropic of Cancer, dots in an ocean area two thousand miles long and fifty miles wide.

The islands, despite their equatorial location, are mild and pleasant in climate, freshened by ocean breezes. Because of their location, their produce, and the friendliness of the people, they soon became a welcome halt for vessels of trade and exploration. English, French, Spanish, American, Russian ships all stopped at Hawaii en route to Canton or other ports and left refitted and refreshed.

The islands and the islanders changed, however. Their Stone Age civilization gave way to the Iron Age. The so-called civilized world, the world of ships and guns, of trade and profit, of nationalism and imperial rivalries, came to bear on what had been a relatively simple existence. The old-time religion and the old forms of government felt the impact of the Western world and changed.

In the late eighteenth century Hawaii was a feudal society. At the top were four kings, each ruling one or more of the islands. At the bottom were the people, attached to the soil and the sea that fed them. They served their chiefs, tending their lands and going to war when called. These local chiefs, frequently ambitious, often resorted to war to gain territory or power. The Hawaiians, of Polynesian descent, were religious people; every important activity started with a religious observance. Their gods personified natural objects and the forces of nature. That is why Captain Cook had been treated with such respect when he first appeared as a godlike figure.

The decentralized political organization was changed by one Hawaiian, a man who was not even in the line of royal succession but who forced his way into it and unified all the islands of Hawaii. He was born on a stormy winter night, probably in 1758, on the island of Hawaii. It is recorded that the wind lashed banana leaves to ribbons that night, and a strange new star appeared in the skies. He was given the name of Kamehameha (The Lovely One). Kamehameha was a nephew of King Kalaniopuu, the king who greeted Cook upon his arrival.

Kamehameha was raised as a warrior. He fought in numerous interisland battles and established a reputation as a good soldier. When Cook arrived, Kamehameha went aboard the ship to inspect it, and one of the English officers later observed that he had "a most savage face."

As King Kalaniopuu grew older, he proclaimed his own son Kiwalao as his successor and named Kamehameha the guardian of the war god. Ambitious, Kamehameha attempted to push himself forward but was forced to retire to the land where he was born. When the king died, however, the local chiefs asked him to be their leader. In the wars that followed he led them to victories on the island of Hawaii. There were ten years of civil war, during which many chiefs attempted to seize power and gain the throne. By 1791 Kamehameha had conquered all his rivals on the island of Hawaii.

Another chief, Kalanikuple, had gained control of Maui, Oahu, Molokai, and several smaller islands. He made alliances with other chiefs and even tried to invade Hawaii, but he was beaten back in a sea battle in which both sides used firearms for the first time. The firearms had been supplied by Europeans. Before then, and to a large extent even afterward, war was fought with spears and slingshots. The men wore helmets made of gourds; their chiefs wore feather helmets; and the priests carried images of the gods into battle. Kamehameha had great success in getting guns from the ships that visited Hawaii, and this, along with his natural abilities, helped him on his road to conquest.

In 1795 Kamehameha was ready. He collected a large army, perhaps sixteen thousand men, and a fleet of war canoes. He captured the islands of Maui and Molokai without too much trouble. His army then landed on Waikiki Beach on Oahu and successfully drove King Kalanikuple's forces back, forcing hundreds over a cliff from which they fell to their deaths. Only the northernmost islands of Kauai and Niihau remained outside his sphere. He tried to conquer them in 1796, but his fleet was broken by a storm. However, the rulers of the two islands later yielded to him, and he became king of the Hawaiian Islands, the first one to rule them all.

As conqueror, Kamehameha controlled everything in the islands. He soon showed that he was as skilled in civil government as he was in war. He divided the lands among his chiefs as a reward for their service, retaining a large amount for himself, of course; he quickly put down crime; he worked

Robert Dampier's portrait of King Kamehameha III as a boy. *Honolulu Academy of Arts / Gift of Mrs. C. Montague Cooke, Jr., Mr. Charles M. Cooke III, and Mrs. Heaton Wrenn in memory of Dr. C. Montague Cooke, Jr., 1951.*

in the fields himself, to foster farming. Fairly soon the ruin of the civil war was forgotten and the islands were prosperous once again.

Kamehameha showed his character when some fishermen who had attacked him during the civil wars were captured. Ten years before, in the thick of the fighting, the future king had landed in a canoe on the Puna coast, and as he ran, chasing some enemy fighters, his foot was caught in a crevice in a lava bed. One of the fishermen had turned back and hit him over the head with a wooden paddle, with such strength that the paddle broke in two. The fisherman ran away. Now Kamehameha was undisputed king and the fisherman was caught and brought to him.

"Why did you hit me only once?" Kamehameha asked.

"I thought once would be enough," the fisherman answered.

Whereupon the king freed the fisherman, gave him some land, and proclaimed a law that became known as "the law of the broken paddle." It said:

Citizens, respect your gods. Respect the big man and the little man. Let the old men, the women and the children walk upon the highway and lie down in the road in peace. Let none disturb them. The penalty is death.

Under Kamehameha, Hawaii flourished. Farms prospered, trade grew, foreign ships flocked to the friendly islands, and Hawaii was starting to become the great melting pot of races and nationalities that it is today. Kamehameha established an absolute monarchy and on his death, in 1819, he passed the crown to his son, Liholiho, who took the name of Kamehameha II.

During his reign the missionaries who greatly changed the life of Hawaii started to arrive. Kamehameha II continued his father's policy of friendliness to the British and in fact went abroad in 1824 to visit England. He died that same year, and the following year his younger brother Kamehameha III became king. Under his rule, a council of chiefs was set up, and in 1839 they produced a declaration of rights and laws that some have called the Hawaiian Magna Charta. Its preamble, reminiscent of the Declaration of Independence, reads:

> God hath made of one blood all nations of men, to dwell on the face of the earth in unity and blessedness. God has also bestowed certain rights alike on all men, and all chiefs, and all people of all lands. These are some of the rights which he has given alike to every man and every chief: life, limb, liberty, the labor of his hands, and productions of his mind.

The first written constitution of Hawaii was signed by the king in 1840. It created a representative body of legislators elected by the people, and also a supreme court. Thus the absolute monarchy of Kamehameha I was transformed into a constitutional monarchy, with the consent of the king.

Despite domestic peace and tranquillity, Kamehameha III now faced danger from abroad. First a French naval ship appeared in July 1839 and threatened to bomb the islands unless an act of religious toleration was passed permitting Roman Catholic missions to operate. The Hawaiians, helpless militarily, complied. In 1843 a British warship presented a series of demands, based on controversial land claims.

"I will attack Honolulu at four o'clock tomorrow afternoon if the demands are not met," said Lord George Paulet, the British captain. The defenseless king thereupon ceded the islands to the British. On February 25, 1843, the Hawaiian flag was lowered and the British flag raised as a ship's band played "God Save the Queen." Just five months later, however, Rear Admiral Richard Thomas, commander of the

British fleet in the Pacific, arrived and corrected the wrong. He ordered the British flag lowered, the Hawaiian flag raised. Hawaii regained its independence, and Kamehameha III resumed his role as an independent monarch.

The United States had in 1842 formally recognized the independence of Hawaii. Secretary of State Daniel Webster said that the United States was more interested in Hawaii than any other nation was, and added: "No power ought either to take possession of the islands as a conquest, or for the purpose of colonization, and no power ought to seek any undue control over the existing government, or any exclusive privileges or preferences in matters of commerce."

In 1843, after the British flag episode, both Britain and France signed a declaration recognizing the independence of Hawaii. After that, it became increasingly clear that the United States was the foremost foreign influence in the islands.

The years that followed were years of economic growth and political ferment. A new constitution in 1852 gave the people a share in making laws. Kamehameha IV, on his accession two years later, pledged to uphold the constitution but soon came to believe that it limited the powers of the king too much. His successor, Kamehameha V, when he became king in 1863, refused to take the oath to maintain the constitution. The following year he handed down a new constitution that, not unexpectedly, strengthened the powers of the king and abolished universal suffrage. When he died in 1873 without having named a successor, the legislature elected a new king, William Charles Lunalilo, who reigned for only a year. On his death, David Kalakaua succeeded him. He was the last king of Hawaii.

An affable, generous man, Kalakaua had only one defect: He believed in the divine right of the king to rule. One of the many anecdotes about him described him playing the game of poker. His opponent showed four aces and reached for the money on the table. Kalakaua stopped him. "Five kings beat four aces," Kalakaua said. "Here are four kings in my hand and I am the fifth." He won.

Two great events occurred during his rule. The first was the signing of a treaty of reciprocity with the United States on January 30, 1875. Under the terms of this treaty, the United States admitted Hawaiian sugar and rice tax-free. In return, Hawaii admitted manufactured goods from the United States without taxation. This treaty brought a tremendous economic boom to Hawaii. Industry flourished; immigrants, mainly Chinese and Japanese, flocked to the islands. The second great event was a reform movement that had some aspects of a revolution. The reformers, mostly white Americans, in 1887 forced through constitutional changes that extended the right to vote and curbed the powers of the king. From then on, tension mounted between the king's supporters and the reformers.

Kalakaua died in 1891 and was succeeded by his sister, Liliuokalani. Fifty-two years old, a strong, ambitious woman, she thought constitutional reforms were an affront to the dignity of the monarch. She had been a social leader in the community, and she was also the composer of one of Hawaii's most famous songs, "Aloha Oe." A figure of great dignity, she had served as regent of the kingdom on two occasions when her brother had been absent from the country. Now she was determined to win back the prerogatives of the crown.

The crisis came in 1893. Queen Liliuokalani drew up a new constitution restoring royal powers of appointment and depriving foreigners of the vote unless they were married to Hawaiians. Her cabinet refused to sign it. The determined queen called out her troops and stepped to a balcony of her palace to address the people. The alarmed reformers organized a Committee of Public Safety and decided to act. On January 16, 1893, they held a mass meeting to denounce the queen.

On the same afternoon the United States minister ordered troops to land from a warship in the harbor, for the purpose, he said, of protecting American lives. The next day the safety committee took possession of the government office building. From its steps a proclamation was read establishing a provisional government. Judge Sanford B. Dole, a leader in the bloodless revolution, was named president. The reformers said they had taken control of the government "until terms of union with the United States of America have been negotiated and agreed upon."

The queen yielded to superior force. At six o'clock that evening Liliuokalani signed this proclamation:

I, Liliuokalani, by the grace of God and under the constitution of the Hawaiian kingdom Queen, do hereby solemnly protest against any and all acts done against myself and the constitutional government of the Hawaiian kingdom by certain persons claiming to have established a Provisional Government of and for this kingdom.

That I yield to the superior force of the United States of America, whose Minister Plenipotentiary, His Excellency John L. Stevens, has caused United States troops to be landed at Honolulu, and declared that he would support the said Provisional Government.

Now, to avoid any collision of armed forces, and perhaps the loss of life, I do, under this protest and impelled by said forces, yield my authority until such time as the Goverment of the United States shall, upon the facts being presented to it, undo the action of its representative, and reinstate me in the authority which I claim as the constitutional sovereign of the Hawaiian Islands.

Thus ended the kingdom of Hawaii. Liliuokalani, the last monarch, had lost her throne in an attempt to regain the actual powers of a queen. She retired to her home in Honolulu.

The Hawaiian revolt was embarrassing to the United States, however. The native, historic government of Hawaii had been overthrown in a revolution led by white Americans backed by the presence of American troops. Now these revolutionists were asking for admission into the United States. Grover Cleveland, then president of the United States, sent James H. Blount to investigate. Blount reported that the monarchy had been overthrown by a conspiracy between the revolutionary leaders and the United States minister to Hawaii. Cleveland acted swiftly. He sent another ambassador to Honolulu, Albert S. Willis, with instructions to restore Queen Liliuokalani to the throne.

Willis asked Dole, president of the provisional government, to resign. Dole refused.

"Mr. Cleveland sees fit to deny our application for unity with the United States," he said. "That decision properly rests with him. But Mr. Cleveland has no authority to interfere in the internal affairs of this nation—nor would Congress support him in any such policy."

Dole was right. Cleveland had no intention of going to war to restore Liliuokalani to the throne. Neither did he have any intention of annexing Hawaii under such circumstances. Failing in their immediate purpose, the revolutionists thereupon held a constitutional convention and established the Republic of Hawaii on July 4, 1894. Dole became its first president.

The election of William McKinley as president of the United

Queen Liliuokalani, Hawaii's last monarch. *The Bishop Museum.*

States revived Hawaiian hopes for annexation. A treaty was ratified by the Hawaiian Senate in 1897. In the United States, though, the necessary two-thirds vote in the Senate could not be achieved.

With the outbreak of the Spanish-American War, however, the strategic value of the islands to the United States was emphasized. A joint resolution of annexation, which required only a majority vote in Congress, was introduced, as had been done in the case of Texas. The resolution was signed by President McKinley on July 7, 1898. The next day the *New York Times* reported:

HAWAII IS NOW AMERICAN

President McKinley Signs the Annexation Resolution
Completing the Work

Admiral Miller to Sail out

The Philadelphia *Will Carry the Flag*
to the Islands—A Commission to be Appointed
Before Congress Adjourns

On August 12, 1898, President Dole and his cabinet walked out on a platform in front of Iolani Palace, seat of the government of Hawaii. The USS *Philadelphia* in the harbor boomed a twenty-one-gun salute, and cannons on shore responded. Thousands of people looked on, but many Hawaiians, remembering Queen Liliuokalani, stayed away. A local newspaper reported: "Precisely at eight minutes to twelve today, the Hawaiian flag descended from the flagstaffs on all government buildings, and exactly at five minutes to the same hour, the Stars and Stripes floated on the tropical breeze from every official flagstaff."

Dole took the oath of office as the first governor of the

territory of Hawaii on June 14, 1900. The new territory consisted of eight inhabited islands and more than a hundred smaller ones, with a total area of 10,932 square miles. The eight main islands were Hawaii, the largest, and Maui, Oahu, Kauai, Molokai, Lanai, Niihau, and Kahoolawe.

Almost immediately, talk began of making Hawaii a state in the United States, but this movement did not become serious until 1935. It grew immeasurably during World War II, when Pearl Harbor became a synonym for surprise attack and Hawaii became a bastion of American defense.

In 1946, after the war ended, President Harry S Truman urged the admission of Hawaii. Congress did not act until 1959, when Alaska and Hawaii were proposed together, in one "admission package." Since Alaska tended generally toward the Democratic party politically, and Hawaii toward the Republican, members of Congress associated with either party saw the logic of joint expansion.

The House Subcommittee on Interior and Insular Affairs, headed by Representative Leo W. O'Brien of New York, took note of Hawaii's distance from the continent and reported, in 1958:

> The argument that Hawaii should forever be denied statehood because their islands are not physically contiguous by land to the continental United States is in our judgment fallacious. It should play no part in consideration of this measure. Hawaii has for many decades been completely incorporated within the American system in every respect despite its lack of land contiguity. It is within the American judicial, customs, and internal revenue systems. Its churches, fraternities, veterans and other organizations, its business groups and banking systems are closely linked with their counterparts on the mainland. In terms of modern communications and transportation, Hawaii is today

far closer to Washington than were many of the Original Thirteen States when the Constitution was adopted. In short, Hawaii is an integral part of the American scene.

With modern methods of transportation and communications—air, sea, radio and telephone—the argument that Hawaii is noncontiguous is purely a technical one. Hawaii is in fact contiguous to the mainland for all practical purposes. The committee believes that the Union of States that is the United States is more than a mere geographic arrangement. It is a union that comes of a common loyalty and a common purpose. In these respects, Hawaii is, in fact, contiguous.

As an example from the past, when California was admitted to the Union, a trip to Washington meant 13,355 nautical miles around Cape Horn or crossing vast, hostile Indian country of the western plains. When the Panama Canal was opened, the voyage by water from Washington to San Francisco was cut to twice the distance from Hawaii to San Francisco.

The Senate approved Hawaii's admission by a vote of 76 to 15; the House of Representatives by 323 to 89. Just before the final vote in the House, white-haired John W. McCormack, Speaker of the House of Representatives, arose, to have the last word in the debate:

"I particularly want to compliment the distinguished gentleman from New York [Representative Leo W. O'Brien] because he, with another distinguished gentleman in the other body, that fine Senator from Montana [James Murray], will go down in history as two men who are the co-authors of two bills admitting states into the Union, Alaska and Hawaii.

"The gentleman from New York and Jim Murray . . . will occupy a place in the history of our country, in my opinion, that no other member of Congress will ever occupy in the future and that no member has occupied in the past. They are the co-authors of bills that became law bringing two separate states into the Union of our country.

On March 21, 1959, President Dwight D. Eisenhower signed the official proclamation of Hawaii as the fiftieth state. A few minutes later William F. Quinn answered the telephone in Iolani Palace in Honolulu. He turned from the phone and announced to the waiting crowd: "Ladies and gentlemen, Hawaii is now a state." Then he took the oath of office and became the first governor of the state of Hawaii.

The next day the *New York Times* took note of the event in an editorial:

THESE FIFTY STATES

A ceremony performed in Washington yesterday afternoon would have astounded the statesmen and politicians who successfully proposed in 1787 the union of these states. There were thirteen then. There were fourteen when the independent republic of Vermont consented to join with the others in 1791. Now with the formal proclamation of the statehood of Hawaii there are fifty.

The Old Thirteen clung to the Atlantic seaboard, looking west into the wilderness that wise men believed might require many generations to settle. Neither the wisest of them, nor the most irrepressible of them, not even Senator Benton of Missouri, who pointed across the great river and exclaimed, "There lies the East, there lies the road to India," ever dreamed that our Commonwealth of States would spread northward to the Bering Sea and westward 2,000 miles into the Pacific. But now it has done these things.

The nature of our union, it may be said, has thus been changed. We are no longer hemmed in by continental boundaries. The racial mixture in North America is unbelievably simple compared with that which has taken place in Hawaii. In Hawaii, east and west, north and south, racial strains that have not previously mingled since the dawn of history are now part of one community. It is our own community now, it is bone of our bones and flesh of our flesh. It inherits the Declaration of

Independence, the whole Constitution, all the great traditions, equally with us.

A Hawaiian is as much a citizen as a Kansan. There are now to be sitting in the United States Senate the Hawaiian-born son of an indentured Chinese immigrant, and in the House, the Hawaiian-born son of a poor Japanese clerk. They need apologize to no one for their background or their parentage. They have, with the rest of us, an equal right to be proud of the word American.

In this small world, Hawaii is closer to the Atlantic coast than Pittsburgh was in 1789. In the words of Edna St. Vincent Millay's poem, there are no islands any more. There is a single continent of liberty.

The fiftieth state may be our final one. Likewise, the day may come when the boundaries of nations and states no longer have a doctrinal significance. But in today's world we feel a little more secure with these Americans on guard, enjoying equal rights with all other Americans, on the Bering Strait and in the mid-Pacific.

13

Islands in the Caribbean

THE USS *MAINE* BLEW UP in the harbor of Havana, Cuba, on February 15, 1898, with a heavy loss of American lives. The cause: an underwater mine. In two months the United States was at war with Spain, though no one was ever able to prove that the Spanish were responsible. In those two months Spain did everything in its power to avoid war. It offered an armistice to Cuban rebels; it indicated its willingness to grant at least partial freedom to the Cuban people. But the United States, inflamed by cries of "Remember the *Maine!*" and newspaper stories of Spanish atrocities, was determined to liberate Cuba by force of arms. On April 18 President William McKinley sent a message to Congress ignoring the conciliatory steps taken by Spain.

"I have exhausted every effort to relieve the intolerable condition of affairs which is at our doors," he said. "I await your action."

Congress promptly declared war, with these words: "The United States hereby disclaims any disposition or intention to exercise sovereignty, jurisdiction or control over said island except for pacification thereof, and asserts its determination, when that is accomplished, to leave the government and control of the island to its people."

The United States went to war gaily. Volunteers flocked to the army in the idealistic belief that they were going to "free Cuba." John Hay, the secretary of state, called it "a splendid little war." Correspondents from the field sent home stories that created heroes such as Lieutenant Andrew S. Rowan, who carried "a message to García" (Calixto García y Iñiguez, the Cuban rebel leader); Admiral George Dewey, who issued the quietly stirring order: "You may fire when ready, Gridley," at Manila Bay; and Colonel Theodore Roosevelt of the Rough Riders, a politician who parlayed disobedience of orders into the presidency.

Spain, a paper power, was unprepared for war. Her navy was badly trained and could not cope with rising United States naval power. Admiral Dewey steamed into Manila Bay in the Philippines at dawn on May 1 and within a few hours destroyed eight Spanish ships—and won control of the Philippines. In the Atlantic too, the American fleet commanded by Admiral William T. Sampson quickly defeated the Spanish.

On land it was different. The United States Army, ill-prepared and ill-equipped, was baffled by such elementary military functions as transportation and sanitation. Thousands of American soldiers died of disease. The Spanish soldiers fought well but were finally overcome by superior American forces. By July the war was over.

The treaty of peace, which was signed in Paris on December 10, 1898, provided for Spain to evacuate Cuba, which would be occupied by the United States. In addition, Spain ceded to the United States the island of Porto Rico (that was its spelling then), the island of Guam in the Marianas in the

Frederic Remington's "Charge of the Rough Riders Up San Juan Hill." Theodore Roosevelt leads the charge on horseback. Remington was a war correspondent who painted the scene as he observed it. *Frederic Remington Art Museum.*

Pacific, and the Philippine Islands. Thus Spain, once a powerful nation, was stripped of her possessions both in the Atlantic and in the Pacific. The United States, emerging as a world power, acquired territories in every direction.

Following is a description of the areas the United States gained then and later in the Caribbean. (The Pacific territories will be discussed in the next chapter.)

Cuba

The United States, in its declaration of war against Spain, had pledged to make Cuba free. Almost everyone in Europe, accustomed to power politics, expected the United States to find a reason to annex Cuba, once the war was over. The

Americans kept their word. General Leonard Wood commanded an army of six thousand men in Cuba for three years, while a treaty was worked out with the rebels. The major feature of this occupation was medical, not military. Dr. Walter Reed led an army team of investigators who in cooperation with Cuban doctors discovered that yellow fever is transmitted by mosquitoes. A vigorous antimosquito campaign wiped out the disease.

In 1901 the Cubans agreed to grant to the Americans rights to use a naval base at Guantánamo Bay for a period of ninety-nine years, a provision that was to embroil the nation in a quarrel with the Cuban government of Fidel Castro many years later. The Cubans also recognized the right of the United States to intervene "for the preservation of Cuban independence" or to preserve order. This controversial provision, known as the Platt Amendment, was revoked in 1934 at the demand of the Cuban government. In 1902 the United States Army left Cuba, and Cuba was free.

Puerto Rico

If there ever is another state in the United States, it will probably be Puerto Rico. Ever since the island was ceded to the United States by Spain in 1898, the question of its status within the United States has been a cause of agitation by Puerto Ricans.

At present, Puerto Rico is a commonwealth, which means that the Puerto Ricans are citizens of the United States, with complete self-government. Although Puerto Ricans cannot vote for president of the United States, they do elect a resident commissioner, who has a voice but not a vote in the House of Representatives. Many Puerto Ricans believe that commonwealth status is the best for them; others want statehood; and some want complete independence.

Puerto Rico is the smallest and most eastern of the Greater Antilles, facing both the Atlantic Ocean and the Caribbean. It is one hundred miles long and thirty-six miles wide, about two-thirds the size of Connecticut. Several offshore islands are part of Puerto Rico; the largest are Vieques, Mona, and Culebra. Puerto Rico is 885 miles from the closest point on mainland United States, southern Florida. Its population of more than three million is Spanish-speaking, with English as a second language.

Before the Spanish came, the island was the home of Indians who called it Borinquen. Juan Ponce de León was the first Spaniard to land there, at San Juan in 1508. Hardship and disease quickly wiped out the natives, and slaves were brought in to do the work. San Juan, because of the favorable position of its harbor, soon became an important shipping point for Spanish galleons carrying gold on the way to Spain from the New World. A plantation economy developed and Puerto Rico settled down to a placid existence.

After the United States gained Puerto Rico, it provided, in 1900, under the Foraker Act, a civil government with an elected assembly and a governor appointed by the United States. In 1917 Puerto Ricans became American citizens, under provisions of the Jones Act. The name of the island was changed from Porto Rico to Puerto Rico in 1932. After World War II, Congress authorized the islanders to elect their own governor, beginning in 1948.

The Virgin Islands

About thirty-five miles east of Puerto Rico lies a group of nearly a hundred islands, the Virgin Islands. Of these, sixty-five belong to the United States, the others to Great Britain. Of the American Virgin Islands, only three are of an appreciable size—St. Croix, eighty-two square miles; St. Thomas, twenty-seven square miles; and St. John, fifteen square miles.

St. Croix was one of the first lands to be sighted by Columbus on his second voyage across the Atlantic. He sailed into the Salt River estuary to replenish his supply of fresh water before sailing on. He named the islands Las Vírgenes, after the eleven thousand virgins of Saint Ursula. In the islands, Columbus encountered the savage Carib Indians, who were unpleasantly cannibal in habit. This discouraged settlement for many years.

During the seventeenth century, many European nations sought to control the islands because of their strategic location and their profitable sugar crops. In 1671 Denmark chartered the Danish West Indies Company and colonized St. Thomas and later St. John. The Danes purchased St. Croix from the French in 1733. The islands remained under Danish control until 1917, when the United States, fearful that Germany intended to acquire them, purchased them from Denmark. The price was $25 million.

The Virgin Islanders are citizens of the United States, with the right to vote in local elections and for their governor. They cannot vote for president of the United States, though, but they do elect a member of the House of Representatives, who may vote in committee but not on the floor of the House.

Navassa

About two miles in area and uninhabited, Navassa rises from the water about a hundred feet, between Haiti and Jamaica. It is mostly exposed rock, with enough grass growing to support a large goat population. By presidential proclamation in 1916, the island is reserved for a lighthouse, administered by the United States Coast Guard.

The Panama Canal Zone

A treaty giving the United States perpetual rights to a ten-mile strip of land extending across the Republic of Panama to build a canal, was signed by President Theodore Roosevelt in 1903. The United States received "in perpetuity the use, occupation, and control of a zone of land for the construction, maintenance, operation, sanitation and protection of said (Panama) Canal" from the Pacific Ocean to the Caribbean Sea. Panama retained "titular sovereignty," words that Americans thought had no practical meaning.

Behind this legal document was a revolution fostered by the United States government. There was no such country as Panama when the negotiations for the canal began. The land was part of the Republic of Colombia, which rejected a proposal by Washington for a one-hundred-year lease of a ten-mile-wide canal zone, in return for $10 million and an annual rent of a quarter of a million dollars. French agents (a French company had begun canal operations but had stopped in 1889 after millions of dollars had been spent and hundreds of lives had been lost), local businessmen, and some United States citizens planned the revolt. By no coincidence, three United States warships arrived off Panama in late October. On November 4, 1903, a provisional government of Panama was

Jonas Lie's painting "Culebra Cut" depicts the building of the Panama Canal. *The Detroit Institute of Arts, City of Detroit Purchase.*

set up without bloodshed. Two days later the United States recognized Panama.

In a short time, Secretary of State John Hay negotiated the canal treaty with Panama in the exact terms that had been rejected by Colombia. The United States was assigned all rights in the zone that it would "possess and exercise if it were the sovereign of the territory." The United States took possession on June 15, 1904, and began construction of the canal, which was opened to traffic in 1914.

Almost before construction began, a controversy arose between Panama and the United States on the precise definition of American rights. Panama maintained that United States jurisdiction pertained only to matters affecting the canal; the United States contended that it had full powers over everything within the zone. In the succeeding years there were several revisions of the arrangement. In 1922 the United States paid Colombia $25 million "to remove all misunderstandings" arising from the acquisition of the zone. By 1955 the United States had raised the annual payments to Panama to almost $2 million, but the ticklish question of sovereignty had not been settled.

After a riot in Panama in 1959, President Dwight D. Eisenhower conceded that "we should have visual evidence that Panama does have titular sovereignty over the region." President John F. Kennedy in 1963 announced that the flags of the two nations would fly side by side whenever the American flag was flown by civilian authorities, mostly Americans working on the canal. Zone residents opposed this policy and decided that they preferred no flag to both flags. This triggered a riot in 1964, when American students tried to raise the United States flag in front of the Balboa High School. Riots broke out and three Americans and twenty-one Panamanians were killed. Panama broke relations with the United States and went to the Organization of American States with charges of aggression by the United States. The dispute was patched over later that year, but no settlement was reached.

It wasn't until 1978 that the dispute was resolved, with the United States yielding sovereignty over the canal. President Jimmy Carter signed a treaty giving control of the canal and the Panama Canal Zone to the Republic of Panama, effective October 1, 1979.

14

Islands in the Pacific

The Philippine Islands

The war with Spain ended in the summer of 1898, and the United States won a full victory. Spain ceded the Philippine Islands, in return for a payment of $20 million. The United States, flushed with its easy victory and full of good intentions, made plans to bring the benefits of American civilization to the islands—and found itself embroiled in another war. The Filipinos, the natives of the islands, wanted their freedom and wanted it right away. They had no interest in seeing their Spanish masters replaced by Americans.

In a speech, President William McKinley expressed the American viewpoint:

> The future of the Philippine Islands is now in the hands of the American people and the Paris Treaty commits the free and franchised Filipinos to the guiding hand and the liberalizing influences, the generous sympathies, the uplifting agitation, not of their American masters, but of their American emancipators.

Until Congress shall direct me otherwise, it will be the duty of the Executive to possess and hold the Philippines, giving to the people there peace and order and beneficient government, affording them every opportunity to prosecute their lawful pursuits, and encouraging them in thrift and industry; making them feel and know we are good friends, not their enemies, that their good is our aim, that theirs is our welfare; but that neither their aspirations nor ours can be realized until our authority is acknowledged and unquestioned. . . .

If we can benefit these remote people, who will object?

The Filipinos objected with force of arms to this patronizing attitude. Their goal was immediate independence. Their leader, Emilio Aguinaldo, issued a declaration of independence, called for a constitutional convention, and organized an army. On February 4, 1899, a bloody war, dismissed in most history books with a sentence or two, broke out. It lasted two years. The Filipinos, lacking arms, equipment, and military discipline, fought bravely but were pushed back from town to town and village to village by trained American troops. The Filipinos resorted to guerrilla warfare, hit-and-run tactics that the slow-moving American army found it difficult to cope with. However, an intercepted letter revealed Aguinaldo's position, and a small American force captured him there.

Young Manuel Quezon, an officer in the insurgent army and, later, president of the Philippines, was sent by the insurgents to make sure that Aguinaldo had been captured. He came into Manila and was conducted directly to the Malacanan Palace, from which the Spanish governors had long ruled the Philippines. It had become the headquarters of General Arthur MacArthur, commanding the American troops. Through an interpreter, young Quezon told the general that he had been instructed by his commanding officer, General

Tomás Mascardo, to learn what the status of General Aguinaldo was. Without a word, General MacArthur pointed to a room across the hall.

Trembling, Quezon walked in. General Aguinaldo was there.

"I have been sent by General Mascardo to receive your instructions whether he should continue fighting or surrender," Quezon said in Tagalog, the native language.

"I have taken the oath of allegiance to the United States and have no right to advise you to go on fighting," the captured general replied.

Thus the insurrection ended. The rebels laid down their arms in 1901, and there began an era of cooperation between Americans and Filipinos that more war, hardship, even torture were not able to break. During these years the Filipinos gradually assumed self-government. In 1935 the islands elected Manuel Quezon y Molina as their first president and became a commonwealth of the United States, with the promise of full independence ten years later.

Relations between the United States and the Philippines were put to the test beginning December 7, 1941, when Japanese planes attacked Pearl Harbor in Hawaii and bombed American airfields in Manila, destroying the United States air force in the islands. The Japanese landed troops on Luzon and pressed toward Manila. Despite a stout defense by combined Philippine and American forces under the leadership of General Douglas MacArthur, son of the MacArthur who had put down the Philippines' insurrection forty years before, the Japanese armies advanced. Bataan and Corregidor became symbolic of courage in the face of defeat.

The American and Filipino armies surrendered, but some individuals and groups continued their resistance as guerrillas, as Aguinaldo had done many years earlier. They waited patiently for the day of liberation. Late in 1944 General MacArthur led a powerful army, navy, and air force back to the Philippines, as he had promised when he left in 1942. The Japanese fought hard to hold on, losing almost half a million soldiers in action, but could not stop the advancing tide of American victory. On February 27, 1945, MacArthur turned over civil rule of the islands to their president.

Despite the heavy loss of life in the war—a million Filipinos were killed—and despite great economic dislocations, the United States kept its promise. On July 4, 1946, the Philippine Islands became independent. The Filipinos retained their ties to the United States by signing a ninety-nine-year treaty granting the United States military and naval bases on the islands.

Over the years, though, the Filipinos gradually began to resent the presence of the United States bases as an infringement of their independence. Following an earthquake in 1991, the United States abandoned one of its major bases, Clark Air Field, which was covered with volcanic ash, and negotiated a closing of its only remaining base there, the huge Subic Bay naval station.

Guam

About six thousand miles southwest of San Francisco, and about fifteen hundred miles southeast of Manila, lie the Mariana Islands. Largest and most populous of these is Guam, a kidney-shaped island thirty miles long and from four to eight miles wide. The largest island in the Pacific between Hawaii and the Philippines, it was discovered by Ferdinand Magellan on March 21, 1521. He named these islands the "Ladrones" (Thieves) because of the habits of some of the natives. The name was changed in 1668 to the Marianas in honor of Mariana de Austria, queen of Spain. In 1898, at the end of the Spanish-

American War, Guam was ceded to the United States. The other Mariana Islands were sold to Germany.

The Japanese invaded and captured Guam in World War II. In July 1944 the American forces heavily bombarded the island, practically destroying the capital, Agaña, before landing and recapturing it from the Japanese. Now Guam is a major United States base in the Pacific. The civilian population is more than 130,000.

Guam is a tropical island covered with tall, graceful coconut palms, broad-leaved banana trees, breadwood, and numerous other trees. Its background of intense green is broken by the brilliant red and magenta of bougainvillea and hibiscus. Its climate is healthful and pleasant, but because it is in the Pacific typhoon belt, it is occasionally visited by severe storms. Typhoon Karen in November 1962 destroyed about ninety percent of the buildings on the island. One official said: "Typhoon Karen was the best thing that ever happened to Guam. It was a massive slum-clearance project accomplished overnight, changing the whole face of the island for the better."

In 1950 President Harry S Truman signed the Organic Act of Guam, which made the Guamanians citizens of the United States. Guamanians cannot vote in United States elections, but they do have a representative in Congress. A member of the House of Representatives, he or she can vote in committees but not on the House floor.

As an unincorporated area of the United States, under the jurisdiction of the Department of the Interior, Guam elects its own governor and territorial legislature.

American Samoa

The southernmost area of the United States and the only U.S. territory located below the equator, American Samoa is in the

Southern Pacific Ocean, twenty-three hundred miles south-west of Hawaii, and sixteen hundred miles northeast of the northern tip of New Zealand. It consists of six small islands of the Samoan group plus Swain's Island to the northwest (included to make its administration easier). The land area of American Samoa amounts to seventy-seven square miles. It is about one-fifteenth the size of its nearest neighbor, Western Samoa, which was formerly administered by New Zealand but is an independent nation today.

American Samoans—there are more than forty thousand—are Polynesian in origin and are among the few remaining societies that retain a major part of their Polynesian customs. The basic economic and political unit is an extended family organization, akin to a clan and administered by the head of the family group, a *matai*. The *matai* is responsible for control of the family lands and property and represents the family in the political affairs of the village.

The first American to touch the islands was Lieutenant Charles Wilkes of the navy on an exploration voyage in 1839. In 1889 the United States, Britain, Germany, and the local government signed a treaty proclaiming the Samoas neutral ground. Ten years later Britain and Germany waived their rights to the islands now called American Samoa. In 1900 President McKinley placed them under the jurisdiction of the United States Navy; in 1951 responsibility for the islands was given to the Department of the Interior.

Since 1977 Samoans have elected their own governor and territorial legislature. Based on legislation passed in 1978, Samoa also elects a member of the United States House of Representatives, who has all the rights of a representative except that of voting on legislation on the House floor.

American Samoa is an unincorporated territory of the United States. The Samoans are nationals (not citizens) of the

United States. They enjoy virtually all the rights of citizens, except that they are not subject to the draft and cannot hold federal office unless they do become American citizens. Many Samoans are opposed to having full citizenship; they think it would destroy their traditional pattern of landholding. Under the doctrine of equal rights for all citizens, they argue, non-Samoan citizens could come in and acquire land, and the communal life of the Samoans would be changed.

The capital of American Samoa is Pago Pago (pronounced *pango-pango*) on Tutuila, the largest of the islands, about twenty miles long and five miles wide. The other islands are Anuu, Tau, Olosega, Ofu, Rose (which is partly underwater at high tide), Sand Islet (only about an acre in size), and Rose Islet (which has neither water nor inhabitants but has the distinction of being the most southern land under control of the United States). Swain's Island, 210 miles to the northwest, was discovered by an American whaling captain named Swain. For many years, in the 1850s, it was occupied by an American family that raised coconuts. In 1925 Congress made the island part of American Samoa.

Wake Island

Halfway between Hawaii and Guam is Wake Island, in reality a group of three islands. Wake Island is the largest, about two square miles; Wilkes and Peale islands are nearby, connected by a roadway. Wake Island was discovered in 1568, rediscovered by the British in 1796, claimed by the United States in 1900, and made a United States naval base in 1934. In the following year a Pan American Airways base was built there.

On December 7, 1941, the Japanese attacked Wake, which was held by a small detachment of marines under the command of Major J.P.S. Devereux. After a gallant defense the marines were overcome and the Japanese captured Wake. Americans bombed the Japanese there during the remainder of the war but made no attempt to recapture the islands. In September 1945, a month after their formal surrender, the Japanese gave up the island.

Wake is now a commercial aviation base administered by the United States Air Force. Its only population consists of air force personnel.

Midway Islands

The Midway Islands take their name from the fact that they are almost at the 180th parallel of west longitude, halfway around the world from the prime meridian at Greenwich. The two small coral islands called the Midway Islands are actually at 177°22′, about twelve hundred miles northwest of Honolulu. The larger island is about two miles long and has an airfield, a cable station, and a lighthouse.

The islands were discovered by an American shipmaster in 1859, and on September 30, 1867, Captain William Reynolds of the USS *Lackawanna* formally took possession. He said that the larger of the two islands was "the first island ever added to the domain of the United States beyond our own shores." The Midway Islands are best known because one of the most famous naval battles of World War II was fought around them in 1942.

The Japanese fleet concentrated its forces in the Central Pacific in June 1942 in a desperate effort to conquer Midway for use as a forward outpost, which would make the United States base at Pearl Harbor in Hawaii almost unusable. The major objective of the Japanese move was to force the American fleet, then still inferior in numbers, into battle and destroy it. Steaming quietly east, the Japanese were unaware that the Americans had broken their secret codes and knew exactly what the plan was. Admiral Chester W. Nimitz, the American commander, waited.

On June 4, 1942, Japanese planes battered the American base on Midway, but the Japanese aircraft carriers were surprised by American torpedo and dive bombers. The Japanese lost four of their best aircraft carriers. The Americans lost the *Yorktown*, but the Battle of Midway marked the close of the defensive phase of the war in the Pacific. The Japanese advance had been stopped. Soon it was to be the turn of the American forces to attack.

The islands are still administered by the Department of the Navy. Their only population is navy personnel.

Palmyra Island

About a thousand miles south of Hawaii lie fifty tiny islets, making up the atoll of Palmyra. Its total area is about four square miles and it has no inhabitants. It was discovered in 1802 by Captain Sawle of the American ship *Palmyra* and so named. It was part of Hawaii for many years, but when Hawaii became a state, Palmyra was excluded from its boundaries. The highest elevation of land is about thirty feet above water, and the islets are covered with a dense growth of coconut and balsalike trees. Palmyra is privately owned, but under the administration of the Department of the Interior.

Kingman Reef

Thirty-five miles northwest of Palmyra is Kingman Reef, small, uninhabited, and unimportant. It was discovered in 1874 and annexed in 1924 by the United States. Although close to Palmyra, it is not considered part of it. Less than half a square mile in area, it is an unincorporated area adminis-tered by the United States Navy.

Johnston Atoll

About seven hundred miles southwest of Honolulu, the Johnston Atoll consists of a nine-mile reef, two natural islands, Johnston and Sand, and two man-made islands, North and East. Over the years, military occupation and construction have altered it so that little of its original natural habitat re-mains. Still, almost two hundred species of fish have been spotted near its shores, sea turtles nest in the atoll, and about five hundred thousand seabirds use it for roosting and nesting. Access is limited to military personnel and the atoll is ad-ministered by the Defense Nuclear Agency.

Baker and Howland Islands

The uninhabited Baker and Howland Islands lie about forty miles apart just north of the equator, about sixteen hundred miles southwest of Honolulu. Both are low-lying coral atolls, about a mile long, providing nesting and roosting habitats for at least twenty species of birds as well as green and hawksbill turtles. They are national wildlife refuges, administered by the United States Fish and Wildlife Service, with visits re-stricted to scientists and educators by special permit.

Jarvis Island

Another uninhabited island, Jarvis Island, is a sandy coral reef in the South Pacific Ocean, about one hundred miles east of Baker and Howland Islands. It is the home of seabirds and shorebirds that use its grasses, vines, and low-lying shrubs to nest and forage for food. Like its neighbors, it is a national wildlife refuge, administered by the United States Fish and Wildlife Service, with visits restricted to scientists and educators by special permit.

The Trust Territory of the Pacific Islands

At the end of World War II the United States became the trustee of ninety thousand people occupying 98 islands of a total of 2,141 in three major chains: the Caroline Islands, the Marshall Islands, and the Mariana Islands. The ocean area where the islands are found is fifteen hundred miles wide and twenty-seven hundred miles long, slightly larger than the United States. But the land area of all the islands, if put together, is less than half the size of Rhode Island, the smallest state.

During the sixteenth century these islands were visited by Spanish, German, Dutch, and British explorers. Spain began to colonize the Marianas in 1668 but failed in the Carolines later because of the resistance of the islanders. Later Germany gained control of the Marshalls and Spain of the Carolines. Following the Spanish-American War, Spain sold the Carolines and the Marianas (except Guam) to Germany. When Japan entered World War I as an Allied power, it occupied the German islands.

During World War II many of the islands were the scene of blooding fighting: Tinian, Saipan, Kwajalein, Peleliu. The United States, which had recaptured many of the islands, retained control until 1947, when they became a trust territory of the United Nations. The United States then became the trustee for the islands under the supervision of the United Nations.

The entire geographic area is frequently called Micronesia,

meaning "little islands." It was formerly administered as four separate political jurisdictions: the Northern Mariana Islands, the Marshall Islands, the Federated States of Micronesia, and Palau.

Since 1986 two of them have become independent nations, the Republic of the Marshall Islands, which includes Bikini, the site of American atomic bomb tests, and the Federated States of Micronesia. Both nations signed agreements, called "compacts of free association," with the United States. That means they have complete self-government and the power to conduct their own foreign affairs but agree to vest in the United States the full responsibility for their defense.

The Republic of the Marshall Islands consists of thirty-one atolls and small islands, with a total land area of seventy square miles and a population of about forty-three thousand. Under the agreement, the United States is permitted to use the Kwajalein Atoll as a missile test range.

The Federated States of Micronesia stretches for eighteen hundred miles north of the equator across an archipelago of the Caroline Islands, about three thousand miles southwest of Honolulu. The nation encompasses four states: Truk, Yap, Pohnpei, and Kosrae. Each state consists of several islands, except Kosrae, which is one island. It has a population of about one hundred thousand.

The third of the four former territories, the Commonwealth of the Northern Mariana Islands (CNMI), became a commonwealth of the United States in 1986, with relations to the U.S. similar to those of Puerto Rico, the nation's only other commonwealth. As a general rule, it means that a person born in the commonwealth is a citizen of the United States but without all the rights of a citizen, such as voting for president.

Located in the Pacific Ocean between Guam and the Tropic of Cancer, the CNMI consists of fourteen islands in a three-hundred-mile-long archipelago, about thirty-three hundred miles west of Honolulu. The major occupied islands are Saipan, the seat of government and commerce, Rota, and Tinian, with a total population of under fifty thousand.

The fourth nation remaining in the Trust Territory of the Pacific Islands is Palau, and it is only a matter of time before it gains its full independence. The governments of Palau and of the United States have signed a compact of free association, similar to that approved by the Marshall Islands and the Federated States of Micronesia, but the voters of Palau so far have not voted in favor of it. Until they do, Palau will continue as a trust territory, with complete self-government.

Palau consists of more than two hundred small islands, stretching for more than one hundred and fifty miles, about four thousand miles southwest of Honolulu and only five hundred miles from Manila in the Philippine Islands. About two-thirds of its population of fifteen thousand lives in the capital, Koror.

The Conquered Islands

For many years the United States occupied and administered several islands south of Japan that it conquered during World War II. According to the peace treaty ratified by the United States Senate in 1952, Japan did not renounce her sovereignty over the islands but agreed that the United States would have the right to exercise all powers of administration over the islands and their people.

The principal islands lie in the Ryukyu archipelago, which curves south and west from Japan to Taiwan. Other less important islands extend into the Pacific as far east as Marcus Island, sixteen hundred miles from Okinawa. The United

States, in recognizing Japan's sovereignty, made it clear that it would not seek permanent possession of these islands.

The best known of the islands is Okinawa, almost five hundred square miles in area, with a population of almost half a million. It was the scene of the last great United States amphibious assault during World War II. American soldiers and marines landed on April 1, 1945, and fought one of the bloodiest battles of the war. The Japanese lost a hundred thousand men; the United States lost fifty thousand men before capturing the island.

Maintained as a military base by the United States for years, Okinawa was formally returned to Japan in 1972. Earlier the United States gave back to Japan three smaller groups of islands: the Bonin Islands, the Volcano Islands (including Iwo Jima, the scene of the famous flag-raising by the marines during World War II), and Marcus Island.

15

The United States Today

IF YOU WERE TO TAKE A TRIP around the United States today, a good starting point would be the easternmost point of the country, West Quoddy Head, Maine (latitude 44°49′ N, longitude 66°57′ W), not far from where the St. Croix River drains into Passamaquoddy Bay. By land and by boat, because a good segment of the boundary with Canada is through water, you would traverse 3,987 miles marking the northern boundary of the United States.

The first part of the trip would be rather complicated, north along the St. Croix, then a short trip on land to the St. John River, then along the St. Francis River, then on a diagonal line to the south. If you keep your eyes above the ground, you will notice that the border runs through the middle of a twenty-foot swath cut through forests.

Through New Hampshire, Vermont, and New York, the border runs along this swath until it reaches the St. Lawrence River. Then down Lake Ontario and the Niagara River until Lake Erie, which washes the shores of Pennsylvania and Ohio; then north along the Detroit River to Lake Huron, around Michigan; to Lake Superior and the mouth of the Pigeon

River. The border curves around the northwest angle of Lake of the Woods in Minnesota (the most northern part of the connected forty-eight states, at latitude 49°23' N) and then to the forty-ninth parallel. From there it is a straight line across the forty-ninth parallel, through North Dakota, Montana, Idaho, and Washington to the Pacific Ocean.

Turning south at Cape Flattery on the Gulf of Georgia, you find the Pacific Ocean rolling along the western border of the country, along the rock-bound coasts of Washington, Oregon, and California, for 2,043 miles.

The southern boundary consists of two parts, the Mexican border and the Gulf coast. The border with Mexico starts a little south of San Diego, California, and extends east below California, Arizona, New Mexico, and then in the Rio Grande between Mexico and Texas for 1,933 miles. At Port Isabel, where the Rio Grande flows into the Gulf of Mexico, the boundary follows the Gulf along the Texas, Louisiana, Mississippi, Alabama, and Florida shore for 1,631 miles.

The eastern boundary, from Florida back to Maine, is 2,069 miles along the Atlantic Ocean.

But even as you end this journey, you have not completed your circuit of the United States. The Geological Survey of the Department of the Interior, which is the authority on all geographical matters (except names, which are decided by the Board of Geographical Names), would say you had traversed the borders of conterminous United States—that is, the lands that touch one another, or the old forty-eight states. Before you still are the two newest states, Alaska and Hawaii.

Suppose you start your Alaskan trip at 54°40', Alaska's southernmost point. Wending your way along the Pacific Ocean, you would travel 5,585 miles before reaching the Arctic Ocean. On the way, as you sailed along the Aleutian Islands, you would have passed the most western point of the fifty states, Cape Wrangell on Attu Island (latitude 52°57' N, longitude 172°27' E), a point even farther west than any part of the Hawaiian Islands.

Alaska's boundary on the Arctic Ocean stretches 1,060 miles. On this part of the trip you will pass through the most northern point of the United States, Point Barrow (latitude 71°23' N, longitude 156°29' W).

Turning south to follow the Alaska-Canada border, you will travel 1,538 miles. Here you will find one of the longest stretches of straight line in any border anywhere in the country, the 141st meridian, which divides Alaska and the Yukon area of Canada, a line extending 647 miles.

At the end of this part of the journey, you take a ship or a plane to Hawaii. There is no way to make a circuit of the islands except by water or by air. The islands stretch across the Pacific in a sort of rectangle two thousand miles long and one hundred fifty miles wide. The state consists of hundreds of islands, only eight of which are inhabited. This trip will take you through the most southern point of the United States, Ka Lae, called South Cape, on the island of Hawaii (latitude 18°56' N, longitude 155°41' W).

The United States does not consist of only the fifty states, however. It includes two commonwealths, Puerto Rico and the Commonwealth of the Northern Mariana Islands, and several territories, the most important of which are the Virgin Islands, Guam, and American Samoa. Each of these territories is a landmark of the United States.

The most easterly territory of the United States is in the Virgin Islands (latitude 18°17' N, longitude 65°28' W).

The westernmost territory is Guam (latitude 12°30' N, longitude 144°37' E).

The most southern territory is Rose Islet, one of the Samoan group. It is a thousand miles south of the equator (latitude 14°32' S, longitude 168°11' W).

If you have traveled to all these points, you will have encompassed the vastness of the United States.

The United States can be measured in many ways, and one of the most important is by its area.

How big is the United States?

There are two ways of calculating the size of the United States. One is by taking the area of the original thirteen colonies and then adding the areas of each of the land acquisitions. The other is by measuring the United States today.

In 1980 the Bureau of the Census did it both ways. It recalculated the area of each of the states by using the latest Geological Survey maps. Then it went back over the territorial acquisitions of the United States and measured them on the new maps. The answer was the same: 3,618,770 square miles.*

Following are the figures for the territorial acquisitions:

ACCESSION	DATE	AREA
Original thirteen	1783	891,364
Louisiana Purchase	1803	831,321
Florida Purchase	1819	69,866
Texas	1845	384,958
Oregon	1846	283,439
Mexican Cession	1848	530,706
Gadsden Purchase	1853	29,640
Alaska Purchase	1867	591,004
Hawaii	1898	6,471

*Source: U.S. Bureau of the Census, *Statistical Abstract of the United States, 1990*, 195, 196.

But for the 1990 census the Bureau of the Census changed its definition of area—and the size of each state and of the United States changed, too. Before the 1990 census the bureau counted only bodies of water that were more than forty acres in size and rivers that were wider than one-eighth of a mile. For the new census it decided to include, regardless of size, all lakes, reservoirs, ponds, rivers, and canals as well as estuaries and coastal waters between the shoreline and the three-mile international limit.

As a result, the water area of the United States grew by 171,602 square miles to a total of 251,082 square miles. At the same time, the land area grew smaller by 2,947 square miles (mainly because some land had been made into ponds and reservoirs or included small bodies of water). And so the United States grew by 168,655 square miles. Its official area is now 3,787,425 square miles.*

Alaska, the largest state, remains the largest and grew the most because of its large and indented coastline. From 591,004 square miles, it has now become 656,424 square miles. Rhode Island, the smallest state, grew, too, from 1,212 square miles to 1,545 square miles. Michigan, which was the twenty-third state in area earlier with 58,527 square miles, jumped in the ranks of the states to eleventh with 96,810 square miles, because it now includes most of Lake Michigan.

(See the following pages for a complete list of all the states and their areas.)

Will the United States grow any more? No one can say, of course. But there are some areas of possible future expansion, specifically regarding the District of Columbia and Puerto Rico.

---

*Source: U.S. Bureau of the Census, *Statistical Abstract of the United States, 1991,* 201.

THE STATES OF THE UNION

State	Source of Lands	Date Organized as Territory	Date Admitted to Union	Order of Admission to Union	Total Area (sq. mi.)	Rank in Area
Alabama	Mississippi Territory, 1798	March 3, 1817	Dec. 14, 1819	22	52,423	30
Alaska	Purchased from Russia, 1867	Aug. 24, 1912	Jan. 3, 1959	49	656,424	1
Arizona	Ceded by Mexico, 1848	Feb. 24, 1863	Feb. 14, 1912	48	114,006	6
Arkansas	Louisiana Purchase, 1803	March 2, 1819	June 15, 1836	25	52,182	29
California	Ceded by Mexico, 1848		Sept. 9, 1850	31	163,707	3
Colorado	Louisiana Purchase, 1803	Feb. 28, 1861	Aug. 1, 1876	38	104,100	8
Connecticut	English charter, 1662		Jan. 9, 1788	5	5,544	48
Delaware	Swedish charter, 1638; English charter, 1683		Dec. 7, 1787	1	2,489	49
District of Columbia					68	
Florida	Ceded by Spain, 1819	March 30, 1822	March 3, 1845	27	65,758	22
Georgia	Charter, 1732, from George II		Jan. 2, 1788	4	59,441	24
Hawaii	Annexed, 1898	June 14, 1900	Aug. 21, 1959	50	10,932	43
Idaho	Treaty with Britain, 1846	March 4, 1863	July 3, 1890	43	83,574	14

State	Source of Lands	Date Organized as Territory	Date Admitted to Union	Order of Admission to Union	Total Area (sq. mi.)	Rank in Area
Illinois	Northwest Territory, 1787	Feb. 3, 1809	Dec. 3, 1818	21	57,918	25
Indiana	Northwest Territory, 1787	May 7, 1800	Dec. 11, 1816	19	36,420	38
Iowa	Louisiana Purchase, 1803	June 12, 1838	Dec. 28, 1846	29	56,276	26
Kansas	Louisiana Purchase, 1803	May 30, 1854	Jan. 29, 1861	34	82,282	15
Kentucky	Part of Virginia		June 1, 1792	15	40,411	37
Louisiana	Louisiana Purchase, 1803	March 26, 1804	April 30, 1812	18	51,843	31
Maine	Part of Massachusetts		March 15, 1820	23	35,387	39
Maryland	Charter 1632, from Charles I to Calvert		April 28, 1788	7	12,407	42
Massachusetts	Charter to Massachusetts Bay Company, 1629		Feb. 6, 1788	6	10,555	44
Michigan	Northwest Territory, 1787	Jan. 11, 1805	Jan. 26, 1837	26	96,810	11
Minnesota	Northwest Territory, 1787	March 3, 1849	May 11, 1858	32	86,943	12
Mississippi	Mississippi Territory	April 7, 1798	Dec. 10, 1817	20	48,434	32
Missouri	Louisiana Purchase, 1803	June 4, 1812	Aug. 10, 1821	24	69,709	21
Montana	Louisiana Purchase, 1803	May 26, 1864	Nov. 8, 1889	41	147,046	4
Nebraska	Louisiana Purchase, 1803	May 30, 1854	March 1, 1867	37	77,358	16

State	Source of Lands	Date Organized as Territory	Date Admitted to Union	Order of Admission to Union	Total Area (sq. mi.)	Rank in Area
Nevada	Ceded by Mexico, 1848	March 2, 1861	Oct. 31, 1864	36	110,567	7
New Hampshire	Grants from Council for New England, 1622 and 1629		June 21, 1788	9	9,351	47
New Jersey	Dutch settlement, 1618; English charter, 1664		Dec. 18, 1787	3	8,722	46
New Mexico	Ceded by Mexico, 1848	Sept. 9, 1850	Jan. 6, 1912	47	121,598	5
New York	Dutch settlement, 1623; English control, 1664		July 26, 1788	11	54,475	27
North Carolina	Charter, 1663, from Charles II		Nov. 21, 1789	12	53,821	28
North Dakota	Louisiana Purchase, 1803	March 2, 1861	Nov. 2, 1889	39	70,704	19
Ohio	Northwest Territory, 1787		Feb. 19, 1803	17	44,828	34
Oklahoma	Louisiana Purchase, 1803	May 2, 1890	Nov. 16, 1907	46	69,903	20
Oregon	Treaty with Britain, 1846	Aug. 14, 1848	Feb. 14, 1859	33	96,386	9
Pennsylvania	Grant from Charles II to William Penn, 1681		Dec. 12, 1787	2	46,058	33
Rhode Island	Charter 1663, from Charles II		May 29, 1790	13	1,545	50

State	Source of Lands	Date Organized as Territory	Date Admitted to Union	Order of Admission to Union	Total Area (sq. mi.)	Rank in Area
South Carolina	Charter 1663, from Charles II		May 23, 1788	8	32,007	40
South Dakota	Louisiana Purchase, 1803	March 2, 1861	Nov. 2, 1889	40	77,121	17
Tennessee	Part of North Carolina		June 1, 1796	16	42,146	36
Texas	Republic of Texas, 1845		Dec. 29, 1845	28	268,601	2
Utah	Ceded by Mexico, 1848	Sept. 9, 1850	Jan. 4, 1896	45	84,904	13
Vermont	From lands of New Hampshire and New York		March 4, 1791	14	9,615	45
Virginia	Charter, 1609, from James I to London Company		June 25, 1788	10	42,769	35
Washington	Oregon Territory, 1848	March 2, 1853	Nov. 11, 1889	42	71,303	18
West Virginia	Part of Virginia		June 20, 1863	35	24,231	41
Wisconsin	Northwest Territory, 1787	April 20, 1836	May 29, 1848	30	65,503	23
Wyoming	Louisiana Purchase, 1803	July 25, 1868	July 10, 1890	44	97,818	10
				Total	3,787,425	

In Congress a bill has been introduced that would admit the District of Columbia to the union as New Columbia, the fifty-first state. At present the city's people—a population of more than six hundred thousand, more than in Alaska, Wyoming, or Vermont—are treated as second-class citizens. They can vote for president, mayor, and other offices, but their budgets and finances are still strictly regulated by Congress.

But the move for statehood is mired in partisan politics. Washington is a Democratic city and if granted statehood would certainly return two Democratic senators to Congress, something that obviously the Republicans oppose. So the prospects of adding the District of Columbia to the union as the fifty-first state are dubious.

In Puerto Rico too there is a movement toward statehood. But there are also moves for independence. At present Puerto Rico is a commonwealth of the United States, which means that it is a territory and that its residents are citizens of the United States without all the full rights of citizenship (see Chapter 13). Periodically the Puerto Ricans vote on the issue, but a resolution does not seem imminent.

As for other areas, the movement seems to be in the direction of international, rather than national, control. The United States, which discovered the continent of Antarctica (Lieutenant Charles Wilkes of the navy, in 1839–1840), yielded its claims, together with other nations, in 1959. The area was declared open to explorers of all nations, without regard to nationality.

With the new frontiers in space, the United States has also taken steps so that discoveries will belong to the whole world, not to any individual country. In 1966 President Lyndon B. Johnson proposed that no nation be allowed to claim sover-

eignty over the moon or other areas in space—an idea that
seems to be generally accepted.

And so it may be that as the frontiers of the world expand,
it will be the flag of the United Nations—not the Stars and
Stripes of the United States—that will fly over the new worlds
yet to be discovered.

A Note on Sources and Bibliography

Many of the books about the geographical history of the United States are far too scholarly for the general reader. But there are a few that are suitable for those interested in more details of how the United States grew to its present size.

Two publications are indispensable for any student of the geographic history of the United States. One is Bulletin 909 of the Geological Survey of the Department of the Interior, entitled *Boundaries of the United States and the Several States*, the latest edition of which was published in 1976. The other is Charles O. Paulin's *Atlas of the Historical Geography of the United States*, published in 1932 by the Carnegie Institution and the American Geographical Society.

Other publications suggested for further reading are these:

Bond, Frank. *The Louisiana Purchase*. Washington: Department of the Interior, Bureau of Land Management, 1959.
Bureau of the Census. *Statistical Abstract of the United States 1990*. Washington: Government Printing Office, 1990.
———. *Statistical Abstract of the United States 1991*. Washington: Government Printing Office, 1991.
Bureau of Intelligence and Research, Department of State. *Geo-*

graphic Notes No. 10: Status of the World's Nations. Washington: Department of State, 1989.
National Park Service. *Overland Migrations West of the Mississippi.* Washington: Department of the Interior, 1965.
Office of Territorial and International Affairs. *Report on Territorial and International Affairs.* Washington: Department of the Interior, 1990.

Among the books consulted in the writing of this one and recommended for the general reader are these:

Bailey, Thomas A. *A Diplomatic History of the United States.* New York: Appleton-Century-Crofts, 1958.
Bemis, Samuel Flagg. *Jay's Treaty.* New Haven: Yale University Press, 1962.
Bowen, Catherine Drinker. *John Adams and the American Revolution.* Boston: Little, Brown, 1950.
Chevigny, Hector. *Lord of Alaska.* New York: Viking, 1942.
Clarke, Dwight L. *Stephen Watts Kearny: Soldier of the West.* Norman: University of Oklahoma Press, 1961.
Classen, H. George. *Thrust and Counterthrust.* Don Mills, Ontario: Longmans Canada, 1965.
Dangerfield, George. *Chancellor Robert R. Livingston of New York.* New York: Harcourt, Brace, 1960.
De Voto, Bernard. *The Course of Empire.* Boston: Little, Brown, 1943.
———. *The Year of Decision: 1846.* Boston: Houghton Mifflin, 1962.
Faber, Doris. *John Jay.* New York: Putnam's, 1966.
Goetzmann, William H. *Exploration and Empire.* New York: Knopf, 1965.
James, Marquis. *Andrew Jackson: The Border Captain.* New York: Literary Guild, 1936.
———. *The Raven.* Austin: University of Texas Press, 1988.
Liliuokalani. *Hawaii's Story by Hawaii's Queen.* Rutland: Charles E. Tuttle, 1963.
Morison, Samuel Eliot. *The Oxford History of the American People.* New York: Oxford University Press, 1965.
Morris, Richard B. *The Peacemakers.* New York: Harper and Row, 1965.

Parkman, Francis. *The Oregon Trail.* Garden City, N.Y.: Doubleday, Doran, 1945.

Tompkins, Calvin. *The Lewis and Clark Trail.* New York: Harper and Row, 1965.

Van Doren, Carl. *Benjamin Franklin.* New York: Viking, 1938.

And the files of the *New York Times.*

Index